ULTIMATE MONEY MINDSET

The 2X Method

A New Entrepreneur's Guide to
Money, Wealth, Freedom and Growth

By

Bill Stacy

ULTIMATE MONEY MINDSET

The 2X Method

A New Entrepreneur's Guide to Money, Wealth, Freedom and Growth

ISBN: 978-0-646-93291-0

Audio-book available at
www.UltimateMoneyMindset.com

CONTENTS

CHAPTER 1

Introduction

Ultimate Money Mindset (The 2X Method) is a brand new guide to (and way of looking at) money, wealth and good living. It's written specifically for entrepreneurs and wealth seekers worldwide and was created with the primary aim of sharing a more effective, more powerful and infinitely more useful perspective on money, wealth and freedom.

It includes a simple formula that you can use for calculating exactly how much money you need to be wealthy, to feel rich, be free and to live a happy, exciting and satisfying life as soon as possible.

For too long one "all powerful" word and symbol has been used almost universally across all nations, societies, decades and centuries to describe wealth. That word is *"Millionaire"*. The 2X Method challenges this simplistic and outdated definition of wealth and proposes a stronger, more useful and ultimately more relevant alternative.

The 2X Formula can be used to gain financial clarity, increase your abundance, attain freedom and achieve faster growth. You (and everyone) can apply it equally no matter which country you're in, what socio economic background you come from (or find yourself in currently) or how much you currently need to live or even how much you want out of life.

I have no problem with having (or wanting to have) millions of dollars and having millions of dollars would obviously qualify you as a wealthy person but what I'm challenging here is the notion that *"you have to be a millionaire to be financially free"*. I say no, you don't and shortly I'm going to lay out a very simple formula that proves this. I believe financial freedom is much closer than many people think and in this book I'll explain why.

This is not a manual on how to get wealthy. It's a manual on how to be wealthy, how to enjoy your current wealth or (if you don't consider yourself wealthy yet) how to recognize when you are and what you need to achieve real financial wealth. Before we get started, I'd like to share a short story of the events that led up to my realization that a wealth formula not only was possible but needed and what elements needed to be include to make it relevant and effective.

Several years ago I started an internet business with two partners. It soon became very successful and soon I was earning a relatively passive $20,000 a month – often more. After just a few short years I was fortunate enough to be offered an extraordinary amount of money for my share so naturally I sold it.

That was a good day because I suddenly found myself with $650,000 cash in the bank begging me to spend it which I did. I didn't spend it all but I spent a lot. I did what most people would do. I enjoyed myself, enjoyed my freedom, played the wealth game, started some new businesses and generally had a great time, but the biggest reward I got was a new perspective on money.

I discovered that I didn't need to be a millionaire to be financially free.

I felt wealthy, I felt rich. I had no financial stress. I could do anything I wanted for as long as I wanted. I could stay up all night and sleep in till midday if I wanted to. Every day was a new adventure in freedom. One day I was bored and felt like doing something exciting so jumped up off the coach and decided to hit the open road on a totally aimless road trip with no goal other than to just enjoy the open roads of Australia's east coast.

For weeks and weeks I just drove up and down in and out of little towns, on big open freeways and barely sealed thin unmarked back roads in a powerful supercharged V8 ex-circuit racing car which was (barely) modified for street use. My only aim was to soak up the road, smiling at the chunky exhaust tone of a hot V 8 and bask in my newfound freedom. For a guy like me who'd previously only known working for a living, trust me when I say, I was living my *ultimate* dream. A billion dollars could not have made me happier, more excited, more satisfied or feeling better about my life.

Now, obviously, many people go on road trips. You've probably been on a few yourself but not many people can say they did it without a care in the world as to the destination or direction. I had no specific destination. I just took turns when I felt like it and stopped and started whenever and wherever I wanted to. Sometimes I'd stop, switch off the engine and listen to the silence.

Other times I'd be driving along enjoying a beautiful winding section and when it ended I'd make a U-turn and go back over and do it again the other way. The outback roads of Australia became my ultimate playground. My only real aim was to find somewhere to sleep for the night. It was total road trip freedom, a real blast and a truly awesome experience.

It's a shame that too many of us live our entire lives not knowing such freedom. I felt like such a lucky guy. I was free and I was enjoying it! I was free from having to go to work, free from worrying about being late, free from worrying about traffic, free from worrying about upsetting my boss. No more scrambling for a car park on a rainy day while running late. No more factories, no more welding bays, short lunch hours or staring at the clock waiting for the end of the day to arrive as the second hand agonisingly ticked over slower and slower.

I was a free man and I realised that although I wasn't a millionaire (not even close), I could finally live the life I'd always dreamed of living; a life of total freedom. It eventually dawned on me that freedom was all I'd ever really wanted. I realised I wasn't running towards being a millionaire as much as I was running *away* from stress, the lack of money and a life that had no real career direction. I had bounced from job to job searching for that feeling of happiness in my work, which I never found.

Up until that point, my choice of careers was largely based on escaping the pain and fear of unemployment and by that I mean I would take any job as long as it paid what I thought at the time was "enough". It seemed that almost every day while I was driving to work (usually at some ungodly hour) I would say to myself the same thing that millions of other workers mumble under their breath every day as they commute mindlessly back and forth to work. You've probably said this yourself...I know I have.

"There must be a better way!"

So I decided to seriously research becoming rich. I did everything I could to improve my attitude and polish my mindset. I read books, I listened to audio recordings, and I attended seminars, visited websites, and joined up for all sorts of things. Sometimes my hopes would be raised as I made some extra money only to eventually spend it all and be back where I started. Making a little extra money gave me the enthusiasm and confidence to keep trying but I never really got "there" – something was missing.

What was missing was I never knew where "there" was. I was missing a healthy and balanced financial mindset. I was fixed on this one goal of becoming a *"millionaire"*, convinced that if I could become a millionaire I'd be free to live my ideal life. I had no idea how much money it would take but I knew that it needed to be *"at least 1 million dollars"*.

I figured that once I crossed that million-dollar mark I'd know how to keep going. I now realise that was backwards thinking. I didn't have a solid plan or any real expectations or belief in my ability to actually become a millionaire.

I didn't have a clue how I was going to get there. All I knew was that wealth started with becoming a millionaire and that was where I needed to be. I knew that unless and until I became a millionaire, I wouldn't qualify to call or even think of myself as "wealthy". However, when I sold my business and was staring at all that cash in the bank I knew something wasn't right. It felt *amazing*, I was energised, I was enthusiastic and I had a certain confidence knowing that I could tackle almost anything financial that came my way. I felt wealthy but I wasn't a "millionaire".

I knew I could walk into any shopping mall and there would be nothing inside any shop that I couldn't afford and this was certainly a new feeling for me. I also knew that I could walk into any car yard and buy any car straight off the lot. Now, for a car guy like me that was huge, but not as big as the realisation that I could also buy a nice comfortable house: CASH!

I don't know what position you're currently in. But most people I know would never even dare to dream that one day they could buy a house with a big bag of cash, yet there I was with a big bag of cash – enough to buy a house. Perhaps even two houses!

There was no doubt that I felt wealthy! I *was* wealthy, I lived the life of a wealthy person, I could buy things a wealthy person could, and yet I was only a little more than half way to being a millionaire. Something wasn't right. This felt *way* better than it should have. How could I feel so "rich" without being a millionaire?

My thinking had been altered and after much discussion and dissection over the last few years, I've come to the realisation that all these years I'd been thinking of wealth in the wrong way. I discovered something extraordinary, something that I would never have discovered had I not been in the position I was in.

By the time you've finished reading this book my hope is that you'll have crystal clear financial clarity. Having clarity around money and wealth by understanding what wealth is and defining it precisely is important because with clarity comes relief, certainty and drive; all essential elements for your journey into wealth and beyond.

When it comes to money, I believe I've discovered a better way to think of and be comfortable with wealth and this book was written to communicate that idea. The "2X Method" is based around a formula for real personal wealth.

Over the past 7 years I've practiced as a wealth and money mindset coach and consultant and (as of writing this book) I've conducted over 800 hundred personal 1-on-1 interviews and mindset sessions with budding and existing entrepreneurs (often lasting for more than 3 to 4 hours) in which I've shared the 2X Formula and attempted to change, improve and update the way they think about money and wealth and what it means in their lives.

I've whittled that experience down to a simple formula that you can use to define wealth in a relative manner. The "2X Formula" (pronounced two "ex" not two "times") will calculate the exact amount of money you will need to feel financially fit, free of financial stress, and to start living a fantastic – perhaps even

AWESOME – life, and all way before you even get close to being a millionaire.

The *"2X Formula"* works by calculating your essential expenses which represent our financial stress. It then allocates a reasonable buffer, which gives us freedom from financial stress, and – presto – we have an exact amount to aim for which will give us comfort, will remove stress and even allocate a reasonable amount for a little fun and luxury along the way as well as allowing for future growth and financial security.

In this book, I explore our desire for wealth, why we want it and what wealth is really all about. I will attempt to offer a simpler, more meaningful and more relevant definition of wealth as well as an alternative, easier way to manage, appreciate and enjoy the real power of money – no matter how much we need (or think we need) in order to be wealthy.

I think we could all do with a fresh new outlook on money and wealth to carry us away from financial stress into the 21st century and beyond.

Chapter 2

The 2X Method
Global Formula for Wealth
(Pronounced "two-ex")

$$2X = F/(H+P)$$

X = Essential Expenses
F = (Financial) Freedom
H = Hobbies
P = Passions

2X in a Nutshell:

All you need is **double** your essential expenses (2X) in income to feel wealthy, have the financial freedom to enjoy your hobbies and passions and live an exciting and satisfying life.

CHAPTER 3

The 2X Method: Explained

This simple yet powerful formula is the only thing you really have to remember from this book. This is your "take away".

It's so powerful because it changes the way we look at money, wealth and freedom and lays down the foundation for a brand new exciting, satisfying and fulfilling life. It's all encompassing and applies to everyone on the planet who's in search of a better life through financial enrichment.

Anyone in the world can use this formula and it will lead us directly to wealth. In many cases quite quickly, and in some real cases – instantly. If lack of money is what's holding you back and you want more prosperity in your life, the *"2X Formula"* will give you a clear and essential understanding of where real wealth is hiding and how to recognise it when you find it.

Think about the minimum amount of money you absolutely need to live your current life and cover your *absolutely* essential expenses. This is your "X" and it's called "X" because the formula needed a variable to account for all the different levels of expenses we face as individuals. The "X" variable is what makes this simple formula work for everyone. This is also why it's called (and pronounced) the two "Ex" method – not the "two times" method. "Ex" also stands for "eXpenses" so it also has a double meaning.

It doesn't have to be exact, but the more accurate you get, the more clarity you'll have and clarity leads to freedom. To make it easy, I'll give you a few suggestions. Most of the people I've given wealth and life coaching sessions to are from the middle-to-lower middle class and, where I'm from, we calculate expenses weekly. So please feel free to adjust this to suit what you're used to.

The formula works for weekly, fortnightly, monthly or even yearly calculations because it relies on variables (X) and percentages. If the math is too difficult to calculate right now don't worry; you can use your current income as X. In other words, instead of trying to calculate which of your expenses are essential just use your current income as "X" and let's double that to get you to "wealth".

While we're talking about mathematics, please don't be intimidated by the formula or calculations. Everything I'll discuss in this book involves halving, doubling or balancing equal amounts so the math is as easy as it gets. It's so simple that young children can understand it.

I'm writing this from my own middle-class perspective, but from all the interviews I've had while testing and fine-tuning this with people from many different countries, I've come to the conclusion that it's safe to say that most people reading this can afford to live in a comfortable suburban house, including all *essential* expenses, for about $1,000 per week.

I know that over time (and depending on where you live and when you're reading this) this will change, but it's a nice round number and it makes the lessons easy so we'll use this figure throughout the book.

If you're making a lot more or a lot less than $1,000 a week, the formula applies just as equally to you. You'll see why shortly. As I mentioned earlier, I've interviewed enough people from all over the world to accept that (at the time of writing this book) $1,000 a week (per average adult) is more than enough to live a very comfortable suburban life.

If you live in a very expensive area like Sydney or New York just double your essential expenses to $2,000 a week ($8,000 a month). When I've suggested this to people who live in Sydney and New York, they seemed happy to accept it as "plenty".

Of course, there are people who need more and people who could live comfortably on less but this is just an average to illustrate the point. Keep in mind we're talking *essential* expenses only at this point. No fun or luxury items are to be included at this stage. And it's important that we define essential and non-essential expenses clearly, for reasons that will soon become obvious. So, let me be absolutely clear by what I mean when I say "essential expenses".

Think of it this way; if you lost all your income, how much money would you need, as a regular income, to avoid being kicked out of your current residence? Many people live in comfortable middle-class houses for quite a bit less than $1,000 a week. That's OK; if that's you, imagine you just got a pay rise to $1,000 a week.

If you're earning (or need) way more than that, just play along, adjust your numbers later and humour me for now by answering "how many people do you think would be able to run a comfortable, urban, middle-class house for $1,000 a week?" The answer I hear most often when asking this question is *"most people"* or *"lots of people."*

For now, I'll use $1,000 a week because I know I'd easily be able to live in a very nice, average, suburban home and maintain expenses for $1,000 a week. I'm using that as my example, but please stay with me. I'll explain when and how to adjust your numbers as we go along.

CHAPTER 4
Essential vs Non-Essential Expenses

It's the money we absolutely MUST have by "Friday" (our essential expenses) that cause the majority of our financial stress. And it's this stress we want to escape from and probably why we want to become "millionaires". We think that by becoming a millionaire, we'll obviously have no financial stress but as you know and as we'll discuss later...that's not necessarily always the case.

Essential Expenses

Remember; "X" stands for essential "eX"penses.

Imagine you have a choice between buying something nice or non-essential (and ending up homeless because you didn't have enough money to pay the rent or mortgage) or paying for an essential expense and remaining housed. If the expense is fun or luxury in any way, it's *non*-essential. I'm not talking about *"essential for a good life"* (that will be covered shortly). I'm talking about *absolutely* essential or life (as you know it) is ruined.

Another clue to a non-essential expense is that it usually makes you smile when paying it because it's usually an expense for fun or luxury..

Here are some examples of ESSENTIAL expenses:

- **Rent or mortgage payments.** Obviously, these are essential expenses but let's not go overboard. Your main house is essential but if paying rent or mortgage on a second holiday home will cause you to lose your primary residence, then it is a non-essential expense – a luxury that you may be able to trim in order to rebalance your life to a 50/50 ratio.
- **Energy** (Electricity and/or Gas, heating...etc).
- **Water**, Rates, Property Taxes & other essential utilities.
- **Basic food.** No ice cream, chocolate or fancy expensive foods, no eating out, no restaurants, etc., just the basic food needed to stay alive.
- **Basic and essential transportation expenses.**
  For this calculation, we're talking about a basic car with roll-up windows and a heater, not a luxury or sports/recreational vehicle. Remember, if it came down to a choice between "keep the extra car and lose the house" or "lose the extra car and keep the house", the decision is clear.

  If you use public transport, buses and trains are essential but taxis (as convenient as they might be) are non-essential (except of course if you have medical reasons...etc.) If it's a choice between paying for a taxi or keeping a roof over your head, it's an easy choice; only one is essential.

- **Insurance.** For most people, house, contents, car and mortgage insurance are essential (if not sensible), while some other kinds of insurance (such as insuring a luxury possession) will belong in the non-essential category.
- **Education fees and expenses.** Obviously, the kids must go to school but let's not confuse an iPad or the latest running shoes with essential school fees and books.
- **Clothing.** You only need to use a little common sense here; buy a new jacket/shoes or little luxury item or becoming homeless? The choice is easy.
- **Payments for debts.** Any debts you have, regardless of their source, are an essential expense. You must make your monthly payments – there is no choice. Being debt-free is not as important as making those payments so making your payments will eliminate your immediate stress and are clearly an essential expense.
- **Internet.** I consider an internet connection an essential expense. Depending on your circumstances – you may not.
- Basic telecommunication expenses. Mobile/Cell phone...etc.

Now, please don't go selling the sports cars, boats or holiday homes just yet. I know we could debate what is and isn't an "essential" expense but I really want you to understand what I mean by essential and *non*-essential expenses because, when it comes to the "X" in the formula it's important to make the distinction between essential and non-essential expenses.

Non-Essential Expenses

You know when you're spending on something non-essential. It feels very different to paying an essential expense. It feels almost cheeky and self-indulgent. We'll discuss how it's perfectly ok to buy non-essential items shortly, but here are some examples to make sure we're on the same page:

- Luxury "anything".
- Restaurants, luxury food items and even ice cream.
- 2nd car or 2nd holiday house payments.
- Entertainment.
- Donating money to charities, helping others...etc.
- Non-essential travel vacations.
- Pay or cable TV.
- Paying down debts.
- Magazines, periodicals, newspapers...etc.
- Savings deposits.

Think of the minimum amount of money you *absolutely* need to just sit at home, eat basic food, stay warm, watch free TV, and not lose your house. Those are your *essential* expenses. For example, donating money to a charity is great but if it comes at the expense of you losing your house (by missing a rent or mortgage payment) or having your energy disconnected by not paying the energy bill, it's not "essential".

Knowing and understanding which expenses are essential is important because they represent financial stress in our lives and it's escaping financial stress that makes up most of our desire to become millionaires, wealthy, rich, well-off...etc. An essential key to unlocking the massive power of "The 2X Method" is in understanding the following simple principle...

"Wealth" isn't measured by how much money you have. "Wealth" is measured by how far you are from financial stress.

This explains why some people are "financially happy" even though they're not what most people will define as being "rich." They're most likely financially happy because they have very low levels of financial stress. The Aim of the 2X Method is to eliminate financial stress and to maintain that stress-free atmosphere as a stable financial platform for future growth. Having a 2X level of income isn't the end of the road though. It's an initial goal or aim.

2X will give you financial relief but it's not enough for you to stop working for a living. That will only come when you accumulate a lifetime supply of cash, a revolutionary concept which I'll introduce and explain shortly. So, now you understand the difference between an essential and a non-essential expense, let me cement it with this little illustration I call the "three pocket" money management system.

CHAPTER 5

The Simple 3 Pocket
Money Management System

Here's a really simple way you can manage your money using the 2X method as a basis for a new methodology. During my consultations, one of the biggest complaints I've heard is this...

> *"I don't have any control over my money! I don't know where it goes, how much I should be saving or what to do with any extra I have left over. I feel lost; I have no idea about money. I don't know how and no one has ever taught me how to "manage" my money."*

I've addressed this with a simple way to manage your income with a method I call "The Three Pocket System".

At the moment, you're probably only just making a little more than you need to cover your essential expenses. For this example, let's assume you're a typical worker making just enough money to live your current lifestyle and maybe a little more. 1X – 1.5X is fairly common.

If that's you, then your first aim is to stabilise your direction and be mindful that your first destination on the journey to wealth is to establish 2X. Once you're at (or even near) 2X, here's a simple way to manage all future income, no matter how much it is.

1. Essential expenses (X) go into your **left pocket.**
2. Then put an equal amount (X) into your **right pocket** for fun and luxury.
3. If you make more than 2X one week, put the rest into your **back pocket** (i.e. the bank, your savings account).

Goal number 1 = Make 2X and split it into 2 pockets.

Goal number 2 = Bank all income above 2X for security.

An easy way to remember it is that "back" sort of rhymes with "bank". Back/bank, bank/back...you get the picture.

You bank the rest for a very rainy day, but more importantly, to build a lifetime supply of cash. We'll get to that shortly, but right now, I want you to pause and imagine a 2X lifestyle.

Using my example of $1,000 a week for "X" ($2,000 a week for 2X), that could mean that you're living in a nice comfortable (perhaps even stylish) suburban house (adjust that to your liking – you might be perfectly happy in an apartment), that all the bills are paid and you have another $1,000 to spend on fun and luxury. Wouldn't that be a great life? The overwhelming reaction I get from people once their eyes are open to the idea is an *"YES! 2X would be a fantastic life!"*

Imagine for a moment that you've paid all your bills for the week and have an extra $1,000 a week to spend on fun and luxury. Why is this important? Why do I mention fun and luxury? Surely being debt-free and saving your money is more important than fun and luxury – right? I don't think it is.

I think we're in this mess exactly because of the guilt we've been made to feel every time we spend on something that's fun or a luxury. To deny our need to enjoy a bit of fun or indulge in a bit of luxury is to deny a basic human desire. With the 2X Method you're allowed and encouraged to spend up to the equivalent of your "X" on enjoying life. You don't have to spend the entire 2nd X on it, but you should feel perfectly comfortable doing so because you're in control now.

You can save it if you like – saving feels great and, in my opinion, is a luxury in itself. There's no denying that having savings in the bank feels good and that's because it puts more distance between you and financial stress but let's just test 2X and see how it feels...

- It allows for (and even encourages) growth
- It's not a "greedy" amount
- It's achievable
- It's exciting
- It's satisfying
- It stops money hassles

It doesn't make you "rich" but it gives you the freedom to think of new ideas and you might be surprised to learn that having 2X feels 99% as good as you might think it would feel to be a millionaire.

2X is for anyone who wants a better life. Let me illustrate what I mean by that. Once during an internet consultation I came across an enthusiastic young man living in a little village in remote India who was online at his local internet café looking for a way to make money to improve his financial situation.

He was pretty desperate but was clearly suffering from *"millionairism"* (a term I'll explain in chapter 15). He kept saying *"I want to become a millionaire so I can help my village and family and friends."* I decided to test him with the 2X method and we talked about his essential expenses, which were (as you would imagine) quite low.

I helped him calculate his "X" and we calculated that his "X" was $250 a month. I asked him "how would it feel to be able to double your essential expenses and be earning $500 a month?" He said *"Bill, I would be dancing in the street and singing songs about you!"*

So you see, it's not about how much money you have; it's about how far you are from financial stress. 2X feels just as good if your essential expenses are just $500 a month, $500 a week, $500 a day, $10,000 a month or $10,000,000 a month.

CHAPTER 6
How to Get to 2X in Just 3 Weeks!

Here's a neat little trick to get you to feel wealth really fast.

Let's say, you earn $1,000 a week and your "X" is $800 a week so that every week you have $200 left over after paying the bills to spend on fun or luxury items. Your income is at approximately 1.25X. You're certainly within your rights to spend that extra $200 every week (and most of us do) but wouldn't it be great if every week you had $1,600 available so you can have a 2X level of income and feel wealthy?

Wouldn't it be great if you could get there this year or sooner so you can feel that special feeling that wealthy people feel when financial stress is far way? Well, you're in luck. It's not only possible, it's relatively easy.

If you're able to restrain yourself; save that $200 every week for just 3 weeks, you'll have $600 in the bank. Now you have $1,000 income and $600 saved – presto, you have $1,600 available every week which is two times $800 (your "X") - 2X! You just got to 2X in just 3 weeks. In other words, you will feel wealthy in just 3 weeks from today. Now that's quick!

Every week you'd have at your disposal twice as much as your essential expenses. Sure, it's not regular income, but it's there if you need it, it makes you feel good and the best part is that just having it there (even temporarily) feels almost the same as regular 2X in just the same way that 2X feels almost the same as being a "millionaire".

The reality is, that every payday after that (providing you don't spend it all), you'll have 2X at your disposal. You'd have $800 available to cover your essential expenses and you'd have an extra $800 to spend on fun and luxury just like you would if you were making 2X income. If you keep saving you can build a "double buffer" of $1,600 in the bank and feel twice as good and you'd be able to spend a little extra every week without ever dipping down below 2X.

Of course, you may not be able to spend it all every week without eventually losing that 2X feeling but it's there creating that special wealthy feeling week after week for as long as you can restrain yourself from spending down to a level that's below double your essential expenses.

In other words, if you build it up to $2,000 you can spend back down to $1,600 and you'll always have that 2X feeling which, while not being true regular 2X, is still a great feeling. Yes, you can start feeling wealthy within just a few short weeks from now, as long as you earn more than you need.

The next step is, of course, to actually build a 2X level of regular income. But for now, you've "arrived" at step 1 and know what it feels like to be wealthy, i.e. not have any financial "worries or stress". Even if you spend it all on the fourth week you'll be wealthy again in three weeks' time.

If you don't spend it all, you'll continue to feel wealthy (i.e. free from financial stress) for as long as you can maintain that buffer. This is worth serious consideration because it's at this point that light globe might start shining above your head.

It might not be immediately apparent how having just one extra pay packet in savings will make you "wealthy", but keep in mind it's the fundamental shift in attitude that comes from embracing this formula and seeing it in cash in your bank account that will make you "feel" wealthy. This is because 2X is enough to relieve you of financial stress.

The concept of having "enough money" might be a bit tricky to get your head around in the beginning, so let me explain how I've discovered a dramatic way to illustrate the concept of having "enough" with a method I call "*Bloody Knee Economics.*"

CHAPTER 7

Bloody Knee Economics

(Part 1)

I invented the "Bloody Knee Economics Theory" to illustrate how the "financial happiness" gauge works. Think of the financial happiness gauge as a scale of 1–10 with extreme financial stress (or minimum financial "happiness") being (1) and zero financial stress (or maximum financial "happiness") being (10).

Now, imagine you're out for a nice walk and you come across a charming old garden with a gravel path winding its way down to a picturesque pond with a bench; perfect for sitting and enjoying nature and the fresh air. You open the gate and casually start strolling down to the bench so you can sit and take in nature at its finest. You walk slowly admiring the garden, trees and flowers. You're so relaxed that you forgot to watch where you're going and you trip over a rock landing painfully on the ground, skidding on your hands and knees.

Little stones are embedded in your knee, blood starts to trickle, and your knee starts to throb and sting. Can you feel the pain? Has this ever happened to you? Can you remember falling over and skinning your knee or your hands? It burns and stings and, for that moment you wish you could just go back in time to stop the pain. Now, focus on that pain while I ask you 3 questions and offer the most obvious answers.

Q1) How soon do you want the pain to stop?
A) *Obviously, immediately!*

Q2) How much of the pain do you want to be gone?
A) *100%! You want it all gone!*

Q3) Once the pain is gone, can it be any "more gone" than gone?
A) *No! Once it's gone...it's gone.*

Bloody Knee Economics
(Part 2)

Imagine we're good friends and I'm ringing you to share the great news that I've just had a massive financial windfall and I'm sharing it with all my good friends. It might go something like this...

> *"Hey! Great news! I finally sold the business!! Got way more than we all expected (way more!) Therefore, I've decided to share my wealth with all my good friends as well. Don't be embarrassed, trust me. It's a drop in the ocean for me, but I've made a little deposit into your account to "share the love." All tax has been paid. Enjoy! Oh and by the way, I'm sending a limo around to pick you up – we're all going out for dinner to celebrate!"*

With a huge smile, you log into your account to discover an unbelievable $500 BILLION in your account! After calling me back, lots of shouting and laughing, you're convinced it's real and you finally get off the phone to start getting ready for what promises to be a great night out with friends celebrating our new found wealth. Let's freeze that moment for examination.

On a scale of 1–10, how do you feel? Normally at this point I'd wait for your answer. Sometimes I get a few 9s because people think it's a trick question but trust me; you'd be a 10 – full financial happiness. I hope you're nodding. Of course you'd be a 10!

The phone rings, it's me again...

> *"Hey, I'm just going to come right out and say it – we made a slight mistake in our calculations. Put the wrong amounts into the wrong accounts. We rang the bank, made all the adjustments and it's all good now. Sorry about that, see ya tonight!"*

You log in again and this time the balance is $600 BILLION dollars! Now you're really blinking fast, you've lost all control of your eyebrows. You have no idea what's going on. You're back on the phone and, after another 20 minutes of explanations, yelling and laughter, you're assured that, yes, you're now a billionaire 600 times over. Let's freeze that moment for examination as well. On a scale of 1–10, how do you feel? 10 – Right? Of course you would. The phone rings and it's me again...

> *"Hey, you're not going to believe this and this time it's actually bad news – it's less. They made a huge mistake but seriously,*

this time I have legal documents to lock it in. It's not as much
as we all thought it was going to be, but it's still something.
See ya tonight!"

At this point you're not sure what to believe. You're grateful for
anything, of course, so you log back in to discover the amount is
now only $400 BILLION. It's yours. This time the legal documents
are finalised and the amount is "locked in". Just to be safe, you
decide to transfer the money into your own accounts. Your life has
just changed forever.

Let's freeze that moment for examination one final time. On a
scale of 1–10, how do you feel; still a 10, right? I mean wow! $400
BILLION! You almost pass out every time you think about it! Isn't
that interesting? I was able to give you an extra $100 BILLION and
you felt no better. Then I took $200 BILLION out of your account
and you felt no worse. Why? Let's compare your financial pain to
the pain you felt in your throbbing bloody hands and knees from
part 1.

Q1) How soon did your (financial) pain stop?
A) *Immediately!*

Q2) How much of your (financial) pain is gone?
A) *100%! All of it! Gone, instantly.*

Q3) Can your (financial) pain be "more gone" than gone?
A) *No! Once it's gone, it's gone.*

If you're like most people I've interviewed about this, you won't
come down to a 9 until about $100,000. Sure, we'd be grateful for

any extra money (we're not greedy), but as far as measuring a large relief spike, you can easily see $50,000 disappearing pretty fast; a car, some payments, a bit of over-spending and it's gone, but $100,000? That could make a big difference. So yeah, your needle would be bouncing off 10 on the financial happiness gauge.

Here's why the Bloody Knee Economics principle is important;

Bloody Knee Economics proves that there is a point at which "enough money is enough money".

We're all raised with a certain level of marketing around us which is aimed at the average expendable income. Advertising companies know we usually only have a small amount of money after paying for our essential expenses, so most products (if they want us to buy them) are priced at levels that we can probably, or nearly, afford. This shapes our desires and we find ourselves desiring "things" we can usually afford so when we suddenly find ourselves in a position of financial excess, we can easily find things to splurge on.

It's certainly true for me that I could probably buy anything I've ever wanted to buy (excluding very extravagant purchases such as yachts, islands, private jets...etc.) for just a few million. However, with $400 BILLION, I'd (obviously) have *way* more than I would ever need.

Granted, the numbers are excessive, but they do illustrate a very important point that is pivotal in the 2X method of thinking.

Using my small success (when I sold my business for $650,000) as an example, I now had created a new gauge on my dash. It had a scale of 1–10 and displayed the distance I was from financial stress; 1 signified I lived in constant stress and 10 being stress-free.

Now that I had that gauge hard-wired into my thinking, I could clearly see what was going on. $650,000 in the bank shot my financial happiness gauge up to a 10 (as you can imagine) but what if I'd only sold for $300,000? Would my happiness gauge still be showing a 10? Yes. Would I still be feeling incredibly good about my financial situation? Yes I would because I was a long way from immediate and current financial stress.

What if I'd received $850,000? Would my happiness gauge still be at a 10? Yes, because again, I'd still be a long way from my current financial stress. I *clearly* had enough; or so I thought but there were two things I had yet to realise and learn.

- **How much money I needed to live a *great* life.**
- **How much money I needed for my *entire* life.**

Now that we have the 2X Formula firmly implanted into our consciousness, we know *exactly* how much money we need to live a great life. We need exactly twice our essential expenses as income in order to *feel* like we have enough to stop worrying. I don't use the word *"feel"* lightly because the point I'm making is that with *"enough"* you can feel the same as a millionaire feels. I know this for several reasons. Firstly, I've known, lived with and had many deep conversations with actual millionaires – they agree with me. Wealth is *all* about the freedom. The main benefit to having enough money is not that you can now go and spend it all. It's that it brings relief from financial stress. The rest is just for toys. I think we all know that money will not bring us happiness just by itself. But why do we feel "happy" when we get money?

I believe it's because we're confusing happiness with relief. The lack of money certainly brings stress. We all feel it no matter how relatively "rich" or "wealthy" we might appear to others (and rest assured there is always someone in the world who will see us as being "richer", "wealthier" or more "well off" than they are – no matter who you are). So, the existence of more money in our lives brings relief from the immediate stress of not having enough to meet our *current* commitments.

Once again, it comes down to those essential expenses that will make us feel stressed if we can't meet them from week to week or month to month. Remove that stress and we feel relief. And with relief the pressure is released and our natural happiness shines through because that is our natural state.

I believe we're naturally happy (with being alive) unless something makes us unhappy, so it's not that we feel happier with more money; it's just that receiving more money moves us further away from our current financial stress allowing us to return closer to our natural state of happiness.

To illustrate how money isn't directly related to happiness I use an example which I call "Rich, Poor, Happy, Sad".

CHAPTER 8

Rich, Poor, Happy, Sad

Imagine a rich person, a poor person and a middle class person.

Can you imagine a "rich" person being happy about something, anything? Sure, lots of things could make a "rich" person feel happy; watching their children playing, being in the company of good friends, starting a new business venture, a beautiful day...etc.

Can you imagine a "rich" person being sad about something, anything? Of course, many things could make a "rich" person feel sad; the death of a loved one, missing the company of good friends, a business deal gone bad, a miserable cold rainy day, a fight with a loved one...etc.

Can you imagine a "poor" person being sad about something, anything? Absolutely, many things could make a "poor" person feel sad; being homeless, feeling hungry, lonely, helpless...etc.

Can you imagine a "poor" person being happy about something, anything? There is no doubt. Many things could make a "poor" person feel happy; bumping into an old friend, watching their children play, a free meal, a beautiful day, new clean, dry accommodation, the generosity of a stranger...etc.

What about the rest of us in the middle; happy, sad? Of course, there are so many things in all our lives that could make us all feel both happy and sad. Money (alone) can't make you happy or sad and money is definitely not the key to happiness.

My Point: If money had the power to make us feel happy or sad, we'd all be happier (because we all have money), and we'd all be sadder (because we all want more money). It just doesn't add up.

CHAPTER 9
How to Measure "Enough" Money

You might be thinking "I can never have enough money!" and I'm not trying to suggest that you (or any of us) limit growth but to spend the rest of our lives on the never ending pursuit of money seems a little exhausting. My point in this chapter is to suggest that there at least might be value in considering the concept of enough – at least for now. The 2X Method now allows us to consider the concept of "enough" in a relative way. It's now possible to measure how much money is enough for today, this week, this year and of course the big one; how much is enough to feel wealthy and be free of financial stress. There are many instances in life when enough is enough. For example;

If you're warm **enough**...*you're warm **enough***.
If you're cool **enough**...*you're cool* ENOUGH.
If you're fed **enough**...*you're fed **enough***.
If you've got a **full** tank in your car...*your tank is **full***.
If you've slept **enough**...*you've slept **enough***.
If you've **outrun** the lion...*you've **outrun** the lion*.
If you've **escaped** financial stress...*you've **escaped** financial stress*.

You can have that same feeling of "enough" by simply calculating your essential expenses and adding a few weeks' worth of savings. Done! Stress minimised. You're far "enough" away from financial stress so it's not a constant worry allowing you to focus on more important and enjoyable aspects of life.

We have realised and now understand where our financial stress is coming from. We know to give it a number and we know to double it for the "accepted" buffer (2X) and we know that this is where we'll find wealth, as rich and satisfying as we ever desired.

I'm not finished yet, though – it gets better. Now that we have a number (*your specific* 2X), we can take this all the way to the end game to create a complete and totally brand new philosophy of money – the concept of a "lifetime's supply of cash".

Imagine having a lifetime's supply of cash! To never have to ever worry about going broke ever again and have enough to cover all our expenses, have more than enough for weekly fun and some luxury and to even have a sizeable stash of cash for emergencies for the rest of our lives. How good would that feel? This is a new concept which I believe not many people have considered is even possible but it is and yes, I have a formula for that too.

CHAPTER 10

A Lifetime's Supply of Cash

(The Financial End Game)

Regular income has the power to bring relief from immediate financial stress. Having an income allows you to pay your bills (which are bringing you financial stress) but you have to keep working at generating more income to keep it coming in (passive income being the exception), but there is only one thing that will bring you true financial security...**CASH IN THE BANK!**

Having enough cash in the bank to live at 2X for the rest of your life is where true financial security will come from.

Income brings financial relief and pushes financial stress away but only CASH IN THE BANK will give you true financial security.

So, at what point would we feel that true and permanent relief? How much money do we need? Relief will arrive when you have enough money so the lack of money doesn't cause you worry. As long as you have no immediate or foreseeable money problems you won't feel financial stress.

Remember: The true measure of wealth is not how much money you have but how far you are from financial stress. So, all we need is *enough* money to keep all the expenses under control and some left over to spend on having a great life. But how much is enough? The "2X Method" states that twice your expenses (as regular income) is "enough"...at least, for now.

Remember back when you discovered you'd become an ultra-billionaire overnight? Did you feel as if now you finally (and obviously) had enough money for the rest of your life? Just imagine that for a second. No one's ever suggested it before because it was probably claimed to be an impossible number to calculate, because everyone's so different and life's expenses are so variable.

Now that we have the 2X Formula and the right mindset, we can calculate it exactly and put it out there as a number we know. I *love* that idea, so let's explore it because I want you to come away with a totally complete new financial outlook.

First I need to make a distinction between financial relief and financial security. Financial relief is temporary. Most of us feel it a bit when we get paid. A 2X level of income will give you financial relief. When I sold my business and was staring at over half a million dollars in the bank and feeling so good I was certainly feeling relief.

That hollow cautionary feeling that I felt when I was suddenly flush with so much cash came from having stress about financial security. I now understand the exact cause of that stress and un-easy feeling. I knew what I had but I didn't know what I didn't have. I mean, I knew I didn't have financial security but at the time I didn't clearly understand what I needed to achieve financial security.

So, what is it that will give us financial security? During my consultations, I've asked this every time and was (but no longer am) surprised at the answers we come up with. I often get answers in the form of a question because people aren't really sure; *"real estate, stocks, a good job?"* It's not obvious because most of us haven't ever been trained in how to manage money, measure wealth or eliminate financial stress.

These things were *never taught* to us in school. We all had to try to figure it out ourselves and many people feel they must continuously keep striving for more and more and more until they died never having enough and the one who dies with the most "wins" – what a load of bull! The answer is right in front of us now and is really quite obvious. I slapped my forehead when it all fell into place for me.

2X will give you financial relief, and if you never save another penny in your life but manage to have a 2X level of income, that would be awesome. However, there's only one thing that will ever give you full, peaceful, financial security – and that's cash in the bank.

So now, let's calculate it. Would you like to know your number? It's very easy. Now we know what 2X is, we can simply multiply that with how long we're going to live. No one really knows of course, but for the sake of clarity and simplicity, let's just say we're all going to live to 100.

The formula for how much cash we need in the bank to have enough for life is very simple and based on the 2X Formula above. You calculate 2X, decide if you'll be happy with it for the rest of your life, add tax and fees, and calculate it based on your life expectancy. Keep in mind also that the older you get, the less you generally need, which goes some way to counteracting the effects of inflation, but if that worries you, then just make your numbers bigger until you're satisfied.

Here's the formula I use to calculate (roughly) how much money might be needed to have a lifetime's supply of cash in the bank.

(100 – Current age) x 52 x "2X"

I'm using 52 because it equals weeks in the year. I use weeks because that's how I've been paid almost my entire working life so I'm calculating 2X as a weekly amount.

Let's calculate it for a 49 year old.
100 – 49 = 51 (years left to "live" if they live to 100)

    x 52 (weeks in the year)

    = 2,652 weeks left to live...

    x 2X ($2,000)

= $5,304,000

If a 49 year old had that much in the bank right now and (for them) $2,000 a week was 2X, they need never worry about money ever again, as they could go to the bank every Friday and pull out $2,000 for the rest of their lives until it finally ran out at the age of

100 years old. Now that's complete financial security. However, let's dig a little further.

Obviously if you're drawing on your capital, it's depleting, which might not worry you, but it might worry the people in your will. The beauty of total security is lack of worry, and for a true lack of worry, you need zero or close to zero risk. When your money is earning interest it's at risk.

It could be argued that even cash sitting in a non-working account carries some risk and that's true, but even carrying it around on you has risk, as does burying it in a box next to an old log under a big black rock. Therefore, I'm happy to suggest that zero-interest bank "storage" is about as safe as you can get. Spread it around among banks to reduce the risk even further.

5.3 *million* dollars is a lot of money, but if we had to come up with a plan to make it and we had enough time (say 10 years), we probably could; with a lot of hard work and some wise decisions. It's also handy to know that if, as a 49 year old if you ever won a lottery of $5.3 million; at least you'd now know what you had in your hands and what it meant.

How about we slice $3.3Million off that goal?

How do we do that? We do that by allowing a little risk to enter the picture. Not too much risk, but would you be comfortable with 5% per annum interest on your savings? I know that's a bit hard to find sometimes (depending on how your local economy is going) but believe me, if you had a million or two to deposit, you shouldn't have too much trouble securing a 5% p.a. interest rate – paid monthly – if you shop around.

I check with my local bank all the time. I tell them *"my friend won the lottery and I'm trying to convince them to live off the interest"* (which always makes their day) and they come back with serious faces and a brochure with a fixed long term interest rate circled for large deposits paid monthly which keeps me happy.

Even if you don't think it's possible right now to get 5% interest from your bank there'll be a safe low risk investment you can make which will return around 5% - e.g. defense housing, government bonds...etc. Check with your financial adviser. When you have a bag of $2million cash to invest you'll find the bank's doors will open very wide for you.

CHAPTER 11
The Magic 5% Rule

I've "discovered" a rule that makes big money manageable within the boundaries of this discussion. It's the 5% Rule and it's very handy to know as it gives you a broad understanding of how to deal with large amounts of money that come into your life. I know I promised only half, double and equal numbers in this book but allow me one more mathematical indulgence.

The 5% Rule is quite simple and its use is for instant and easy income calculation from big money and it goes like this; the *amount* of millions invested at 5% p.a. interest is (roughly) the same *amount* of thousands you'll earn in interest per week. It's the same first number.

$1,000,000 deposited @ 5% p.a. = $1,000 per week.

$2,000,000 deposited @ 5% p.a. = $2,000 per week.

$3,000,000 deposited @ 5% p.a. = $3,000 per week.

$5,000,000 deposited @ 5% p.a. = $5,000 per week.

$10,000,000 deposited @ 5% p.a. = $10,000 per week.

$38,000,000 deposited @ 5% p.a. = $38,000 per week.

And so on... Interesting and easy to remember, isn't it?

Test yourself. If you won a $3 million lottery, what would you do with it now? I'm guessing that before being exposed to 2X thinking, you might have started to list all sorts of seemingly "sensible" investments or even extravagant purchases you would have made, but now I'm hoping you'd say...

"Throw it in the bank and live a great life off the interest!"
Remember: The Interest IS The Win!

The interest *IS* the "win". The capital should *never* be touched except in an emergency like a dire health issue or kidnapping! OK, I'm only (sort of) joking about kidnapping (I hope that never happens to you) but you know what I mean. A "bargain" is *never* an emergency. A "good investment" is *never* an emergency.

I know it might be tempting to spend the money you're saving to build up a lifetime's supply of cash on these things but that's what the "2" in 2X is for. If you want to have some fun or enjoy a little luxury you can do it out of your right (fun and luxury) pocket or if you don't spend it all every week you can save that but you never (ever!) spend the money your saving for a lifetime's supply of cash until it's a screaming emergency.

Remember, if the interest on your savings is giving you 2X, that's a beautiful thing. Imagine if you couldn't touch the principle and could only ever get the interest as income, and that income was 2X or beyond, wouldn't your "money happiness gauge" be at a 10 – the highest level? I know it would be for me.

Now, I'm not suggesting that making a few million dollars is going to be a walk in the park. It's not. But many people make a LOT more than that and still feel like they have to keep on working because they often drag the expenses "lion" along with them wherever they go – constantly living in fear of it catching up to them and "biting them on the bum".

I can tell you, that if I was ever in a position to cash out of a successful business with a few million dollars I'd put it straight in the bank. At 5% interest I'd be able to live off the weekly income forever, never having to ever worry about money again and neither would anyone who was a beneficiary of my trust – my children, for example.

In fact let's look at my big win when I sold my website for $650,000. If I knew then what I understand now I'd have seriously considered putting it all into a bank account, secured a 5% return and I'd have a $650 dollar a week income *for the rest of my life*. I'd *never* be broke (for more than a few days) again. Or if I ever did spend all my money I'd only have to wait for Friday to get another $650.

Sure, inflation and taxes would eat away at it but that's no different to being on a $650 weekly wage. Inflation and taxes eat away at that as well. At the time of writing this book if I was to seek employment as a welder (my old trade) I'd probably (at current rates) make about $650 a week anyway.

$650,000 in the bank at 5% would create your very own personal retirement "pension". Or if you need more, then you just make more but these numbers aren't anywhere near millions. Imagine if you *were* able to come up with a plan to actually make enough money to be in a position to bank a million dollars.

I was at the bank the other day and I asked for their over-the-counter rates for a million dollars deposited long term with the interest paid monthly and it was 4.85%. Close enough but what if it was only 3.85% – that'd still be $38,500 per year or $740 a week. Before the internet came along I'd never had a regular job that paid me even close to $740 a week so I know from my own direct experience that I'd be able to live very comfortably on that.

I often get asked how to make a large enough amount of money to bank and live off the interest and it's a good question obviously. Most of us are "flat out" making enough to live on, let alone being able to make 2X. Let alone make enough to bank a lifetime's supply of cash. But you and I are not ordinary people, are we?

We're entrepreneurs and we're on the lookout for a way to become "millionaires" – right? Well, 2X offers a methodology to make best use of the extra income that we're about to make. 2X thinking will provide a solid and sensible platform upon which to build your fortune.

I'm guessing that if you're the type of person enjoying this book you're already working on "your first million" and probably planning for many more, am I right? You're into self-improvement and personal development mentally, financially and even spiritually.

There are brand new millionaires surfacing daily. It's been estimated that in 2014 over 500,000 new millionaires were "minted" in the U.S. (40,000 brand new millionaires were "minted" in Australia). I can't see any valid reason why you can't be one of them if you really put in the effort required.

You're thinking about making money, taking steps to make it and even developing a better attitude towards it (proven by the fact you're reading this book). The message I'm trying to get across to you today is that on your way, put some thought into banking and securing some of that extra cash you're making so that you never lose the fortune you make (like so many others have). You've heard the horror stories of fortunes made then lost – don't become a wealth statistic.

Now that you have a "2X" mindset (an ultimate money mindset) you can think like a "brillionaire" (a word I made up to describe someone with copious amounts of brilliance) on your way to becoming a "millionaire". You now have the mindset that understands and appreciates how powerful money can be and how simple and easy it will be to secure your future given your impending wealth.

When people ask me what "I do" I tell them I'm a *"Financial Entertainer"* because I like to spread this new money mindset in an entertaining way. Or I call myself a *"Wealth Therapist"* because I sometimes consult with people who (perhaps like you) are already earning 2X and didn't know it – so I fix that and send them happily on their way with a *brand new and "ultimate* money mindset". But the way I prefer to summarise what I do as this; "I prepare active entrepreneurs for impending wealth".

You want wealth, riches and money – right? Well, now, instead of just running after "more money" without a clue as to how much you want, how much you need, what to do with it when it arrives, you now know exactly how to behave when fortune finds you. And it will.

Now that you have the choice of a new perspective on money, I'd like to talk in a broader sense about what this might mean to you in your life moving forward. By discussing and sharing 2X with so many people before you, I've been witness to hundreds of reactions and further discussions about this, including, of course, how to get 2X.

I often hear *"I love 2X but I don't know how to make more money."* I'm not going to address how to make money here as that's not the purpose of this book. Suffice to say that if you really want to make more money, you'll find a way. I can almost guarantee you that.

You may already be on your way and now that you have a better understanding of how money and wealth works you may find that financial freedom is much closer than you thought anyway. The trick (if there is one) is to be very clear as to what we want and then remove the restraints holding us back. Here's a clue; it's mostly "our own attitudes". For the most part we are the ones holding ourselves back. So, what now? I hope you'll agree that these concepts can help to create a remarkable change in your life, so let's explore them a little further.

CHAPTER 12

How Cool Is 2X?

2X can come from various sources and even though the quality of your life will be instantly improved just by understanding, appreciating and accepting 2X, there are various levels of quality in my own mind which you may or may not share. You can come up with your own definitions of what "quality of life" means to you but take my word for it...2X is cool!

I sometimes use this small story in my personal consultations to illustrate my point of how awesome 2X can be and what it might feel like to suddenly have it. I spent the first 20 years of my working life in many casual jobs, mostly as a welder, truck driver, factory worker...etc. In fact, I counted all my jobs once and it worked out that, over that period, I had been employed in over 65 different jobs. It's the nature of a casual worker. I've only ever had a small handful of permanent jobs with paid vacations and "security."

The rest have all been week-to-week, sometimes just one day or until the job is finished, which accounts for the high number. So

I'm going to use an example of a normal factory worker for this next story because it's a life I know and am familiar with.

Imagine you've been working for a company on the factory floor for some time. You don't hate your job but there are definitely other things you'd rather be doing most days. One afternoon you get called up into the office and invited to sit down with your manager. Three other high-ranking managers have also arrived for the meeting. Something is definitely up. Your manager notices that you're slightly nervous and assures you that nothing is wrong. In fact, they're quite impressed with your work. This makes you relax (and think *"well, give me a raise then"*) and you begin to assume a more relaxed and casual seating position.

For the next few minutes your manager explains how they've been watching you, and that they're impressed with your performance and dedication to quality. In particular, they want to thank you for the suggestion you made at a meeting a few weeks earlier.

The other managers from head office all pitched in to agree and pointed out that your suggestion substantially improved the efficiency of the entire operation, so they've called you in to express their gratitude. You get a warm feeling and try not to smile too widely.

You're informed that the company has decided to share some of the money your suggested efficiencies have made for the company in the form of a raise and promotion! They confirm your current salary (which at the time is less than $1,000 a week) and all look at each other.

"We're going to more than double your salary to $2,000 a week on one condition if you agree. The condition is that you must be the first one in and the last one out which includes Saturday mornings." You agree without a moment's hesitation.

$2,000 a week! Some people never even dream of earning that much and you can barely believe what you're hearing. A few extra hours work is nothing to pay for such a massive income increase.

Your mind is flooded with ideas and you imagine scenes of what your life is going to be like but you see one of the head-office guys smile and wink to your manager. What comes out of his mouth next was the last thing you expected to hear.

> "We're only joking. You don't have to work the extra hours at all. It was a test and you passed. In fact, we don't even need you to come in early when the factory starts. You can come in at 9 and leave at 5 like the office staff and still receive the increase to $2,000 a week. Do you agree?"

"Yes! Of course I do and wow! Thanks!" you say.

Not only are you about to be showered by a waterfall of cash but your work life is also going to become much easier. Whoever hears of things like this happening? You're not quite sure what to think. This is new ground for you and (because you're such a modest person) you're a bit embarrassed. You thought you were just making a suggestion. No one really expects their suggestions to be taken seriously...do they?

You look around the room and sure enough, an even broader smile starts appearing on another manager's face and, while staring straight at him, you see him give a knowing wink and slow nod to your manager.

You dare not wish for better news. But sure enough, your manager drops his head and raises it slower with a massive smile and informs you that they were still joking.

In fact, the *real* deal was that you no longer had to come into work – at all! You would be issued with a brand new fully equipped and set up laptop and could now work entirely from home. But it had to be eight hours a day, monitoring the line and submitting summary sheets and production reports.

All you can do at this point is blink and smile. "Are they serious?" you thought. "No more early mornings dragging myself out of bed. No more being late, no more cold early mornings. I'm free to work from home? It's like a dream come true, but a dream I never dared to dream so even better! Wow, $2,000 a week and work from home?!"

Of course you agreed and couldn't stop thanking them. It was a little embarrassing. What a day! Hold your horses, accompanied by open laughter from the other managers who were all clearly enjoying themselves for some strange unexplained reason. They explain; as it turns out, your "little" suggestion has been implemented and you've made the company millions and millions of dollars.

You were reluctantly starting to allow yourself to wonder (and get a little excited about) where all this was heading. Could it be that the news would get even better? Why were they "playing" with you in such a good way? They continued...

"Here's the real deal. We've created a special app for your smart phone and all we expect from you is to check it once a day to view the reports from yesterday and send them through to us by pressing "OK" or adding notes for our attention. You can do this from anywhere in the world, and yes, we'll still be paying you $2,000 a week. We're really very grateful."

OK now this was serious. This meant you could work not only from home on a fantastic new salary, but that you could do it from anywhere in the world. Totally unprepared for this eventuality, you're at a total loss for words. They ask if you agree.

You do... But of course, they're not finished with you yet. By now, they're all laughing and you're laughing (nervously) and you have to ask if they're serious or are they just playing games? Your manager glances at his laptop, presses a button and the printer whirs into action. He hands you the print and there it is, a deposit into your account of $10,000. *"What's this?"* you ask jovially.

"That's your bonus and here's the real deal. No more jokes, you've suffered enough. We're actually retiring you, effective immediately on a $2,000-per-week pension for life. Four million dollars has been transferred into an account and a 5% interest rate has been locked in long-term."

With the $4,000 a week that'll be earning in interest, we'll pay your tax, transfer $2,000 a week into your account and keep the rest. This way it'll work as a life-insurance policy for your family if you die, so they can continue to enjoy the $2,000 a week.

We thank you for your excellent suggestion and we wish you all the best. All we ask is that you send us postcards and allow our photographer, who's waiting outside, to take a few photos for the company magazine. We want to use you as an example to others."

Wouldn't that be an astonishingly comfortable place to be? Wouldn't you feel proud and safe? I know I would.

CHAPTER 13

How Does 2X Really Feel?

It could be hard to imagine how massive an effect living at 2X would have on your life. Imagine the lifestyle; you could travel, save, have all the modern conveniences you've ever wanted, you could enjoy your hobbies full-time, indulge your passions no matter what they are.

You could help people, give to charities and (within reason) spend impulsively on things that make you happy – even if temporarily – when the urge takes you. And if you spent it all and were temporarily broke, all you'd have to do is wait until Friday for the next $2,000. But you're not a millionaire, are you? Not by a long shot.

What are we talking about here; a hundred grand a year? That's not even 10% the way to millionaire! In some circles that could be defined as a failure to succeed because you didn't achieve "millionaire" status – but not for us. It's hard for me to imagine a better life. Can you feel the shift in perspective that 2X has given you? That's what I'm talking about.

The only financial danger you're in is perfectly within your control. If you want to experience true financial relief it's simple; you must live well within your means (this is old advice) but what this means in our modern lives is simple.

Never spend more than half of your income on essential expenses.

It's a simple and easy rule to remember. As long as you maintain that 50/50 ratio or better, you're OK. This is why 2X works for people of all income levels. If you have an income of $1,000 per week you can arrive at 2X simply by keeping your essential expenses to less than $500 a week. It might be hard but if you really want to achieve it it's not impossible.

If you can't get it down to 2X, you might be able to achieve a better X factor of maybe 1.5X. For most people the way to 2X will be up. Finding ways to make extra money to reach 2X is a short journey. Much shorter than trying to be a millionaire, that's for absolute sure. Imagine the effort it's going to require to become a millionaire.

You might already have thought of it and may even have already started travelling down that road. That's awesome that you've set that goal and like I've said before there's nothing wrong with being a millionaire or even wanting to be a millionaire.

I know that if I had secured a lifetime's supply of cash and had millions left over and could safely spend millions without the risk of moving back into a financially stressful state I'd be having a ball. If that's your journey I wish you luck but don't forget that the feeling of wealth you're seeking will arrive much earlier.

The green grassy field of financial relief, security and safety will arrive a long time before you become a "millionaire" and my task here is to simply illuminate and give you the travel brochure for your journey. In this brochure I've pointed out that there are many beautiful scenes along the way.

I'm sometimes asked, "is 2X anti-wealth"? No, 2X is not anti-wealth. 2X is pro-wealth. I have absolutely no problem with anyone earning any amount of money. In fact I want us all to have lots of money. Not only to buy cool things but to also have the capacity to help others. There are lots of people who really need our help and we need to be financially buoyant ourselves to be able to help others.

Here's where I think society's traditional money mindset has been going wrong...

Think of the normal way our wealth grows. Let's take a nice pay rise as an example; say an extra $100 a week. Previously, that may have been enough to start considering an immediate upgrade in lifestyle. It would have been reasonable to consider moving into a nicer apartment, slightly larger house, take out a new loan to travel or buy a new car or a plethora of other ways we can think to spend it. $100 a week, $400 a month, that's a decent payment on something nice or a decent upgrade in living conditions.

But can you see the problem? If we do that, we're simply dragging our X up every time our income increases. That's why we're always stressed about money, even when we just earned more. We're adding unnecessary financial stress to our lives when the better course of action is to use the extra income to build a buffer, to feel more comfortable by trying to move the balance more towards achieving 2X ASAP.

Buying thicker stronger boots to walk over the same hot sand keeps us in the hot sand. We need to head for the cool green grass and shade so we can get relief from the burning sun of financial stress, so we can cool off, take a deep breath and think about our next best move. Then – and always with 2X in mind – you can grow, always maintaining that 50/50 ratio. Just make sure your essential expenses don't exceed more than half your income.

Maintain a 50/50 ratio between essential and non-essential expenses and you'll always feel wealthy.

CHAPTER 14

Beyond 2X

Let's examine the journey to 2X and beyond. Is it essential to make a lifetime's supply of cash? Is it bad if you don't ever save a single cent? Is it bad to carry debts forever? Well, it depends on your goals, aspirations and achievements but let's just take it one step at a time. Let's say you only ever managed to achieve a 2X level of income and never managed to save an extra cent.

Would that be such a bad thing? I don't think so. I think financial freedom is the first aim followed by personal (time based) freedom. Using the calculations in this book you can now calculate exactly how much money you need for several different time frames. 2X on a weekly basis (in the form of a regular income) will give you temporary relief. It will give you relief for today, this week, this month or this year or for as long as you're making 2X.

Achieving 2X on a weekly basis will alleviate financial stress on a weekly basis but it won't give you a lifetime's supply of cash and if you're not earning it passively (or even semi passively) you'll still have to go to work to earn it. You'll still have debts and you'll still have the worry of having to continue working to earn and maintain a 2X level of income.

However, 2X gives you options. With the spare money (in your right pocket) you have the power to change your life in many ways. You can pay off your debts with it. You could invest it in small business or you could just save it to build a large buffer which could eventually lead to having a lifetime's supply (never ending stream) of cash. A few people have expressed concern about carrying debt and not ever paying it off.

2X and Debt

Firstly, debt is not as big a worry as many people make it out to be. The big worry is making the payments. This is what bothers most people about being in debt. The payments reduce your expendable income but with 2X that's not a problem because you have enough to make your payments and enough to spend on fun and luxury and for you it might be fun or "a luxury" to use that extra cash to pay off your debt. This is OK – do it if it makes you feel happy.

It feels good making extra payments and reducing debt but don't forget that most people (perhaps not you – but most) enjoy only a very brief amount of time debt free before they go straight back into debt so being debt free isn't always the ultimate goal.

The ultimate goal is to become free from financial stress so as long as your left pocket is handling the payments ok then being in debt is not really a problem and shouldn't be a major source of financial stress. *Payments* are the problem. Making the payments on debt is the *real* source of financial stress. So don't worry about being in debt because you may never be out of debt and that's not necessarily a bad thing. Worry about making the payments.

Think of 2X as a beautiful, green, shady, grassed area that's only just above your current level – up a small hill. Compare that to trying to become a "millionaire" which is a very difficult and large task and more like trying to build a mountain. 2X is nice and comfortable; you know exactly where you are and where you're going financially and the view up on your little hill is much better already. Once you're at 2X income and more comes your way, you can think of reducing your debts, but this time with financial comfort and control.

Another problem with debts is that some are so large that you may not pay them off for decades (e.g. mortgages...etc.). If you remain in financial stress while doing that, it seems like a waste of life to me when you could have had the debt for life but you'd never be stressed about it. Because even though you didn't make enough money to pay it off, you were at least living fantastically (I call 2X at any level fantastic) while paying it off. The first and most important step is to gain control over your financial stress.

This is usually by aiming to increase your income to 2X. If you have to work more to do it and you're comfortable with that – great. It might mean starting a small side business in your spare time to make that little extra to get to 2X. The problem I see with too many small businesses is that there is great pressure put on them to turn into a multi-million dollar business when it would be much easier to put less pressure on them by using them to just create enough extra income to make 2X.

However if they start to grow and really take off you can then start your journey to saving enough to build a lifetime's supply of cash.

There are many paths up this mountain and sometimes you may find yourself back tracking or a little bit lost but with the new 2X perspective you'll at least know what you're trying to achieve.

If you remember that achieving and maintaining a 2X level of income feels almost as good as you'd feel when you become a millionaire you'll know that even if you never manage to become (what most people define as) a millionaire at least you'll have achieved financial freedom, clarity and strength. This is a worthy aim and should become your primary focus. What happens *after* 2X is slightly less important as *achieving* 2X.

2X is the ultimate goal. From there, you can stretch and reach to any heights you desire. Just don't forget to always maintain 2X no matter what your income level. If you earn more, always make sure you never spend more than half on your essential expenses and you always use the extra double to enjoy your life and take some time out for fun and luxury.

Conversely, if circumstance finds you in a position where you're making less, simply adjust your essential expenses where you can (it's not always easy) so that you maintain a 50/50 ratio of essential expenses and expendable income. This way, no matter what you earn you'll always feel wealthy and financially free from stress.

Being wealthy or rich or whatever you want to call it is a state of mind, not a specific figure or amount of money or income. You will always be financial free if you learn to control your essential expenses. This is the key to financial freedom. Becoming a "millionaire" is great but it's not essential for financial freedom. This is the most powerful shift in mindset that you can make and it can be made right now. Just by instantly changing your perspective you can achieve the ultimate money mindset and it can happen in the blink of an eye or the creation of a thought. All it takes is to decide to live a 2X lifestyle from now on and you can make that decision right now – if you want.

CHAPTER 15

2X is The Cure for "Millionairism"

Millionairism is a "belief disease" where people have the false belief that they need to become a millionaire in order to achieve financial freedom.

The 2X Method proves that's not the case at all. Financial freedom can be attained a long time before you become a millionaire. In fact, even becoming a millionaire doesn't guarantee that you'll have financial freedom. The 2X Method defines a new and more relevant way of calculating financially freedom.

I want to be a millionaire. Of course I do, and I'm sure you do too. Very few people wouldn't. But I'd like to do a lot of things, and many of them will happen way before I ever make another million dollars let alone have a passive million dollar income. If we're not careful, "millionairism" can be a soul crushing disease because a million dollars is so difficult to make and (even if you do) so easy to lose.

It's absurd that one single solitary exactly-defined amount of money (one million dollars) is the exact same amount that everyone on the planet needs to feel free. Too many people associate this amount with financial freedom and that's just wrong and needs to be addressed.

The way I see it, there's nothing wrong with having (or even wanting) lots of money, as long as you don't deliberately hurt anyone while you're doing it. I think greed is a word that's used too often by people with personal or political agendas. Greed isn't about how much money you want. You're only greedy when you decide it's ok to hurt people for the sake of making more money.

If you deliberately set out to hurt people in order to make money then you're greedy, regardless of the level but you're not greedy just because you have money or want more money. We all have money and we all want more. Does that mean we're all greedy people? No, of course it doesn't.

For example, if you're an inventor and you invent a really cool thing that everyone loves and buys, (or you're an author or a recording artist ...etc.) and you suddenly you have millions of dollars in the bank, does that make you greedy just because all of a sudden you have more than other people? Of course it doesn't. If that were the case, we would all be greedy because we all have more money than someone else.

Greed is defined by your actions, not your possessions or your desire for abundance. Abundance is natural and we could do a lot of good with an abundance of disposable cash. With enough money we could all fix the world, or at least our own little worlds. Who among us wouldn't want so much money that it would give us the power to remove financial stress from friends and family or people we care about?

The danger is in the thinking that *"only by being a millionaire will I be free."* You're on the right track but the numbers are wrong. Having no financial problems is the first freedom you want. Once you've taken care of your own freedom you'll find that your spare time will probably create lots of good ideas that may eventually go on to make you even more millions.

The desire to become a millionaire is fine and there's nothing inherently wrong with it, but the thinking that it's the <u>only</u> way to become "free" crushes your soul because it's such a massive task. I'm not saying it's impossible, but as we've already established, it's not essential for financial freedom.

You can cure yourself of millionairism right now by altering your thinking. It can happen instantly right this very second with a fresh new perspective on money, wealth and freedom.

Side note: **Redefining "Millionaire"**

I apply the strictest rule to the use of the term "millionaire" and my rule is this. I think I should have at least one million dollars *in income* (after tax) to spend, before I call myself a "millionaire".

It's pointless having millions if you can't spend it or use it for some good. Having a million dollars in real estate is fine but it doesn't mean you're a "millionaire" in the way most of us define it.

But if I have a million dollars and spend it, what was the good of that? I like to go even further and say that, unless I have a million dollars in expendable and *replenishable* cash reserves after essential expenses, I wouldn't qualify as a millionaire.

While we're on the topic, let's assume that, in order for people to refer to someone as being a millionaire, you'd need at least one, preferably two million dollars, but if you have more than (say) five, what happens then? Society will refer to you as a multi-millionaire.

That's fine, but the next level after that is billionaire (i.e. 1,000 million dollars). That seems a bit high to me. How can a person with "just" a few million be in the same financial "class" as someone who's worth $800 million?

We need a new class of millionaire and I propose **"Ultra-Millionaire,"** which could be used to refer to people with more than 10 million (liquid) dollars or a double or triple figure millionaire.

I know it's not important but I believe the distinction is useful so I just wanted to put it out there.

CHAPTER 16

Don't Drag The Lion!

The ancient Greek philosophers first argued that our decisions in life are strongly influenced by our desire for pleasure and our fear of pain. Anthony Robbins more recently suggested that we're driven more strongly by the fear of pain than we are attracted to the desire of pleasure. So, if running away from financial stress can be likened to running away from a lion chasing us, once the lion has stopped chasing us, we can relax; we can stop running. We fear the pain of attack no more.

With enough money to live a nice, comfortable, stable life most of us are really happy. What does that say? I think it says that (for the most part), we are good, reasonable people who aren't driven by greed. We're driven strongly by a natural attraction to security and safety, fun and luxury. Even if the luxury we seek is the luxury to be able to afford to give to and help others.

Financially speaking, our most pressing issue is that we just want the financial pain to stop. That's why we feel a little "relief" on paydays (masquerading as happiness). The money eases the pain temporarily. But here's the problem; every time we make more money, we usually spend it. Or worse, we commit it to more debt or essential expenses such as moving into a bigger, nicer house or apartment or, we buy a nicer more expensive car...etc.

To extend the metaphor, we *"chain ourselves to the lion"* (financial stress) and financial stress is ever present as we drag the lion around with us wherever we go. The Lion is always chasing us, always threatening us – causing us stress. Have you ever heard of or met "rich" people who still have financial stress? If not, trust me, they exist. But how could that be?

They make millions and yet they still stress about money? Why? It's because they're *"dragging the lion"* and are always increasing their expenses as soon as their income increases thereby increasing their financial stress every time they increase their income. They may never escape the drudgery of financial stress if they don't unchain their "lion".

This is a big problem and easy trap to fall into because we all want a "better life" as soon as possible. The simple solution is to freeze your current lifestyle (or at least bring it up to an acceptable minimum and then freeze it), define it as a number (X) and lock it in. Don't increase your lifestyle every single time your income increases. Instead, use any extra income as a way to put more distance between you and the financial stress of the bills. Use extra income to build a bigger stronger buffer between yourself and financial stress.

The more you make, the further away you get from stress until soon (at 2X) you realise there's no more financial stress. Everything is well in hand. All your expenses are being covered and there's plenty left over for fun and luxury. What could be better than that? What I've just described is a millionaire style of life – and look how cheap it actually is. That's why I say *"financial freedom is closer than you think!"* You just have to define it. Once you get to and stabilise at 2X, you can grow to anywhere after that. The beauty of 2X is that it brings the millionaire feeling into the reach of everyday people like us.

If you use my four-week wealth plan, you can literally feel the same as a millionaire does in four short weeks! Sure, they might have cooler "things" (don't worry, your time is coming soon), but apart from that, the feeling is the same. I know this because I've felt (and feel) it.

CHAPTER 17

The Greatest of All Human Desires

If I was to ask you "what is the greatest human desire?" what would your answer be? Before you answer, there is a simple rule to apply – it *must* apply to all humans and be at the *top* of everyone's list. If you can think of even one person for whom this would not apply then it's not the *greatest* human desire. I believe, there's one thing that's at the top of the list for us all.

Is it making money? Let's apply the rule; can you think of even one person for whom making more money is not at the very top of their list of desires? The answer is yes because there are many people who don't have the attainment of riches (money) at the very top of their list, so it's not that.

Is it respect? Absolutely not; it might be for some people but not for ALL people so it's not respect. Is it growth? Nope, I know plenty of people who are very happy exactly where they are living their comfortable lives, so it's not growth. It might be for some people, but not for *every* person. Is it prestige? It might be for some – but again, not for all.

This greatest human desire must be at the top of the list for *everyone* and there's only one thing at the top of everyone's list and that's freedom.

Greatest Human Desire #1:
FREEDOM

Freedom is the one single thing that's at the top of all our lists – every single one of us living on this planet – with no exceptions that I can think of. Think about it. Can you think of even one person for whom freedom is not the most important thing? It might not be financial freedom but it'll be freedom from something; freedom from a horrible boring job, freedom from stress, freedom from poverty, oppression, hate, prejudice, discrimination…etc.

We all want freedom and it's the very top of our lists. What's the second most desirable thing in our lives? It's the desire to hang out with cool people and by that I mean hang out with people who we consider cool, not necessarily rock stars, movie stars or people that society considers "cool".

Greatest Human Desire #2:
Hang Out With "Cool" People!

Once we attain our chosen level of freedom I'd argue that the next thing most of us want to do is spend it hanging out with (who we consider to be) "cool" people. Our friends, our peers, our mentors and our families; cool people means all the people we enjoy spending time with. But getting back to freedom; what do we do with our new-found and unexpected freedom? Do we retire to Florida, The Bahamas, Tahiti, the Gold Coast of Australia or move closer to the equator for the nice warm weather? Perhaps, but for most of us, we're too young (at heart) to give up on life that easily; the first thing we do is what I call *"The Flop."*

CHAPTER 18
The Flop

"The Flop" is a state of financial relaxation that you will encounter as soon as you reach 2X from passive income. Active income means we have to actively and constantly work to achieve a 2X level of income. Passive income means we have 2X coming in from sources that require no or very little further effort.

For example, you might be receiving 2X in the form of interest payments from savings in the bank, royalties or sales from a book or income from a business that runs itself with very little input from yourself...etc. You may or may not be a millionaire with passive 2X, but for the most part you're free of work and have enough money to be free of financial stress. This will cause you to do "the flop" – don't worry, it's a good kind of flop.

The "flop" is what we do once we've attained 2X. I'll explain. Think of a marionette which is a puppet controlled from above with strings connected to a wooden frame held in the hand and controlled by a puppeteer's hand movements. Imagine that marionette is you and the strings making you move represent what you must do for money in order to survive.

If the "mortgage or rent string" pulls, you have to move. If the power bill starts pulling, off you go to work to pay the power bills...etc. Our lives can become (and remain) a series of forced movements based largely on our need for money.

Everything from dragging ourselves out of bed in the morning to staying at work for long hours and putting up with people we'd rather not deal with. But what happens when you achieve full passive 2X? Since "X" covers all your living expenses you don't *have* to do anything for money anymore.

The puppeteer no longer has control of your movements and so what happens when you cut the strings on a marionette? It flops to the ground. The human equivalent of "the flop" is what would happen to our daily schedule if we didn't have to go and do things for money, i.e. nothing – at first. If you suddenly found yourself without the need to be active to make money you'd probably do nothing for the first few days or weeks – maybe even months.

When I sold my business and suddenly found myself with plenty of money, my financial stress immediately disappeared so what did I do? To be honest I slept in and watched pay TV for a few months. It took me that long to get it "out of my system". Then I jumped up off the couch drove around Australia for a few months in a high powered ex-racing car just enjoying the road, the solitude, the ultimate freedom and of course the sound of a high performance car.

So much of what we do in our lives revolves around earning money that we've become used to it. It's become a habit and, at first, you may not know what to do with yourself so you "flop" down on the lounge. You have no choice because there's very little left for you to do with your day.

Do you know what you would do if you didn't have to work for money anymore? You might be a bit bored, which is great (and much better than being stressed) because when you're bored it makes space in your life for more new and exciting possibilities to materialise. Imagine jumping off that couch with a big smile, all excited because you just had a great idea.

2X will give you more of those opportunities, days and experiences. You're now free! What are you going to do with it? The world is your oyster! As they say, you can do anything you want, for as long as you like with whomever you want. Freedom is a wonderful thing.

OK, so I'm sure you're convinced already that freedom feels great and that 2X will give you that freedom. But how do you actually live a life of freedom filled with hobbies and passions? If you don't have to go to work, what do you do? First I'd like to discuss hobbies and passions and why they feature so prominently in the 2X formula.

CHAPTER 19
Hobbies & Passions
(It's what 2X and life is all about!)

During the early days after selling my website and having all that disposable cash, I discovered something quite interesting while I was trying to figure out the best way to spend it. I wasn't quite sure what I was supposed to do next with my life, so I just floundered for a while until I realised something. The best things to do are the things you love doing – right?

I discovered that there are really only two categories of activity left after the need for money-making has disappeared; enjoying your hobbies and indulging your passions but what is the difference between a hobby and a passion?

Hobbies:

Hobbies are things you do mostly (but not always) by yourself, for yourself. Hobbies usually make you smile when you think of or are doing them. These are not hard and fast rules – just the way I look at life after 2X. Some of my current hobbies are; collecting, building and modifying old cars and hot rods, playing guitars, creating digital art using Photoshop on my computer, hanging out with cool people and my newest hobby...cooking!

Passions:

Passions are things you do usually with, or for, other people and they don't necessarily make you smile but often give you a deep sense of satisfaction. I like hot rods and old cars with big fast engines. If I was left to my own devices, I could happily tinker with old cars by myself for unlimited amounts of time. Hot rods are my hobby.

Sure, I can get passionate about my hobby, and there's often a crossover between hobbies and passions. But I think that passions are different from hobbies and it's hard to spend all your time just indulging yourself with hobbies because, as humans, we really do have other basic human needs such as the need to contribute to society, the need for personal growth...etc.

This is usually where passions come in. Hobbies are pretty self-explanatory but passions need a bit of further definition and exploration. Imagine you've sorted out your finances and now you have 2X passive income and have all day every day to spend as you wish. You might want to spend your time (and even some of your fun and luxury money) helping people who are less fortunate than you. That's a passion but it's not really a hobby, is it? You're not always smiling but you are enjoying a feeling of immense satisfaction.

Spending time with your family would be a passion. You might spend it together with them enjoying hobbies or following passions, like contributing to your local community, church or school. My passion is improving people's money mindsets by sharing this 2X Method of thinking. Even if I had billions of dollars in the bank earning millions in juicy weekly income I'd still enjoy sharing this message.

To experience the "perfect day" simply combine your hobbies with your passions.

A way I could mix my hobbies and passions would be to drive a radical hot rod all across the US and Australia with speaking engagements at seminars as my weekly destinations. I'd just drive around or head off to my next destination and then speak at seminars, while living in five-star resorts – all within my 2X budget, of course. During my private coaching sessions I came across a guy who really got this point. Here's what he said...

"Bill, I know exactly what you mean! My hobby is playing soccer. I love training, I love practising my ball skills and I love playing games. I love following my team and I love watching games on TV. It just gives me a real thrill. My passion, though, is helping under-privileged kids. It's just so easy to help kids. They're always so grateful and I love it.

I recently experienced a perfect day and it's only just now that you've explained it to me that I realise it. I organised a soccer match for a group of under-privileged kids and it was just the most fantastic day! It was exciting and satisfying and I felt fulfilled as a person. I can't wait to do it again."

By combining his passion (helping under-privileged kids) with his hobby (soccer), he was able to experience the perfect day. Life could not get better for him than doing something he loved with and for people he cared about. During my coaching sessions, many people have had to rediscover their hobbies. They weren't sure what they were or even if they had any. They hadn't stopped to enjoy a personal hobby since they were young. A few said they didn't have any hobbies, and if that's you, don't worry – you'll find some.

You may have to go back to when you were a child ("what did you really enjoy doing as a child?"), but it's there, lurking in the background, buried deep down inside and if it's not there, if you can't find an old hobby, just imagine how much fun you're about to have finding a brand new interest or hobby. Tip: Collecting something is usually a great start.

To find your passion, just think of what you would do if you won a trillion dollars and had bought everything you could ever want. What would you then do to make the world a better place? If you can't think of anything, then think of it as a fantastic opportunity for you to explore the world and all it has to offer. You'll find something that really excites you sooner or later. Jump up off the couch and look into it or go and do it.

If you still can't think of something you're passionate about, that's cool. Try going out and just giving away money to homeless folks or try volunteering where you're needed. You have enough now (even at 2X). Go and help someone. There are people all over the place who need your help right now.

Whatever you choose to do, one thing's for certain; all you have to really do to feel fulfilled is to satisfy two basic human desires in small doses every day. I call this the *"Shot Glass Method"*.

CHAPTER 20

The Shot Glass Method

(The Real Secret to Daily Fulfilment)

OK, so you've got a great life, living on a 2X income and the bank is starting to fill up with your savings...now what? Tim Ferriss (in his excellent book *The 4-Hour Work Week*[1]) raised an excellent point about the purpose of setting and achieving goals, because apparently according to people he polled, that's what made life "great." I'd like to further explore this idea but first, here's what Timothy said...

> *"Let's assume we have 10 goals and we achieve them – what's the desired outcome that makes all the effort worthwhile? The most common response is what I would also have suggested five years ago – Happiness. I no longer believe this is a good answer. Happiness can be bought with a bottle of wine and has become ambiguous through overuse. There is a more precise alternative that reflects what I believe the actual objective is.*
>
> *Bear with me. What is the opposite of happiness? Sadness? No. Just as love and hate are two sides of the same coin, so are*

happiness and sadness. Crying out of happiness is a perfect illustration of this. The opposite of love is indifference and the opposite of happiness is – here's the clincher – boredom.

Excitement is the more practical synonym for happiness, and it's precisely what you should strive to chase. It's the cure-all. When people suggest you follow your "passion" or your "bliss," I propose that they're, in fact, referring to the singular concept – excitement. The question you should be asking isn't, "what do I want?" or "what are my goals?" but "what would excite me?"

Thanks Tim, you make an excellent point and given me food for thought. Is the answer to a great life to just do exciting things all the time? I think I would find it a bit exhausting to be excited all the time and I'm sure the message here could be to find joy in the daily excitement of life, so I'm going to make it a more complete rule by adding a second element – **satisfaction.** But how often do we need to feel excited or satisfied? This is a great question. I believe we live daily. Today is what matters most. Sure, tomorrow is important but today is urgent, and "urgency trumps importance".

If you can spend just a small part of your day doing something exciting and/or satisfying, you're living as full a life as you ever possibly could.

We need excitement and/or satisfaction daily. Further, I think that the key to having a great life is 2X income and something exciting and/or satisfying. But why do we need daily excitement and/or satisfaction? I believe excitement and satisfaction are like vitamins. Just as vitamins are essential to maintain good health; *excitement and satisfaction* are essential to maintain general happiness but you have to keep taking vitamins just like you have to find excitement and/or satisfaction daily.

Imagine a small shot glass with *"The Good Life"* printed on it like a logo. All you need to do is fill your shot glass with one shot of either excitement or satisfaction daily to feel like you're getting the most out of life. You might have two or more shots of excitement in one day, and we often do, but I believe all you'll ever really need to feel "full" is one. There's no need to spend all day on a constant high of excitement or satisfaction. Just one "shot" will be enough.

I believe we should measure our lives by how much we do, not by how long we live or how much we make, and a "shot glass" a day of something exciting or satisfying is enough for us to feel like we're leading as full a life as we can each day. Let's put it to the test and see if it explains some (previously) puzzling human behaviour.

Does it explain why some people don't feel the need to search for ways to make money constantly? Yes, it does, because they're probably getting their little shot of excitement or satisfaction in other ways. Let's look at some people and see if they live (or lived) their lives using their own form of the shot glass principle.

Mother Theresa; did she live her life drinking from the shot glass of satisfaction or excitement? Probably a bit of both, like all people, but I'd guess for her it was mostly about the satisfaction of helping people. What about a skydiver or an athlete? I'd guess mostly excitement with some satisfaction at the end. What about teachers? Most teachers work for the passion of teaching.

Why do "rich people" still teach? Could the Shot glass theory also explain why some "rich people" stop to help and teach others? Do you think just because they have lots of money that they don't need a shot glass of excitement or satisfaction every day just like everyone else? They get it from teaching and helping people. Money has very little to do with why they teach. Sadly we know this because teachers are for the most part poorly paid. They obviously enjoy sharing and teaching and probably will forever. It's inherent in who they are.

Some small thinkers wonder (sometimes out loud), "If someone is so rich, why would they sell me a course or book on making money? Surely they'd just be off enjoying their riches and not worrying about me – right?" This kind of thinking makes them doubt that money making guides have any value, so they miss out on the opportunity to gain knowledge from people who are willing to teach them. If you think of this from a shot-glass perspective, you'll see it makes perfect sense that someone would stop and teach (no matter how "rich" or "poor" they are). They get a deep sense of satisfaction and possibly some excitement as well as some extra income. It makes perfect sense.

**Teachers like to teach. Helpers like to help.
It's what they do. Money rarely changes that.**

When you achieve 2X (and I believe you will quite soon), you're not going to just sit at home and watch TV all day, every day, forever. You might for a while, but eventually you'll set a new direction for yourself and head off again, all excited about your new project. Why? Because the enjoyment of excitement and the fulfilment of satisfaction are almost drug-like in their power to drive us toward our goals.

We all need to drink a "shot glass" of excitement or satisfaction every day in order to feel good about our lives, no matter how much money we have, or even if having large piles of money isn't important to us. Even if it's just doing a good deed or making an anonymous contribution, it will fill you up. Are you starting to get the picture? You can start living like that right now, can't you? It's all you'll need to feel like you've lived a good life that day, as you lay your head on your pillow at night.

For example, I'm involved in internet and information marketing and there are many short courses on ways to make money by successfully marketing goods and services online. Many of these short reports and courses can be read, understood and even acted upon in one day, but too often we hear of people who don't follow through on every single course they buy. The Shot Glass Theory explains this behaviour perfectly.

Let's say a person with a winning attitude decides to educate themselves and they buy a short course on how to make money. If you're an entrepreneur like me you'll know what I mean. We would obviously get excited that day (filling our shot glass with excitement) but the next day we might not follow through, often resulting in feelings of inadequacy... *"Why can't I follow through?"*

What's happening here? There's a conflict. How can something be so great one day and be totally abandoned the next? How does the "Shot Glass Theory" help us understand this common behaviour? Consider this; when we buy the exciting new money-making course that night, are we excited? Yes. Let's agree that our shot glass was filled (with excitement) and consumed that night, but what about the next day?

Given that we need a fresh shot glass of excitement or satisfaction each day, can you imagine *anything* that might come along in our life that next day that might fill the shot glass with something else exciting or satisfying (that day) that's NOT related to the course we bought last night? Easily – right? Does this mean we aren't committed? Of course not; it just means we live life on a daily basis. What was important yesterday might not be important today and that's OK. Has life been reduced to a series of accomplishments as the only measure of quality?

I believe that's a flawed way to live and I'll discuss goal-setting shortly, but can you see why it's perfectly valid for them to have bought the course (it filled them with excitement for a day), and that it's also perfectly reasonable and understandable why they didn't follow through with it the next day? Something else might have happened the next day that filled their "excitement Shot glass". I believe each day is a universe unto itself and each day requires a fresh dose of excitement or satisfaction and that's all it requires to live a great life. This is why it doesn't really matter how much you achieve or when you achieve it. It really only matters that you live as full a life as you can every day.

Do you know for sure that you'll wake up each morning? Do you have the same control over your life and reactions when you sleep as when you're conscious? No. Lots of people die in their sleep. Lots of people die every day. You might die tomorrow. So live for today and worry about tomorrow... tomorrow.

I think striving to fill your daily shot glass with some excitement or satisfaction is enough of a life goal for anyone. Any further growth, excitement or satisfaction for that day (two exciting or satisfying things might happen in one day) is just a "cherry on top" and makes life interesting – but it's not essential for that feeling of fulfilment. That's why some people are very happy with their lives just the way they are. Do you know anyone who's seemingly enjoying their life but is not frantically doing everything they can to become a "millionaire"? I'm sure you do – in fact that describes most of us doesn't it? As long as we get a daily dose of excitement and or satisfaction, then (rest assured) we're living a full life.

There's no need to achieve mighty things every day to feel fulfilled. There is satisfaction in moving toward your goals but relying on the achievement of goals can be dangerous to daily satisfaction and will only rarely feed daily excitement, so I propose we consider re-assessing the importance we attach to setting and achieving goals.

CHAPTER 21

The Astonishing Power of ASAP Goals!

Goals are great, aren't they? Are they or aren't they? What is this love/hate relationship we have with goals? I used to be a goal touter and faithful believer in setting goals in every sense of the word. I was almost addicted to it. It gave me such a rush when I decided how I wanted things to be.

Setting goals requires faith and having faith can sometimes be fully satisfying. So much so that the mere act of discovering, formatting and documenting a particular goal is often so satisfying that it's a complete activity on its own. I rarely achieved many of those big goals, but I had a great time documenting them. Other times I achieved things on such a high level there's no way I would ever have set the attainment of such a high goal. I wouldn't have the cheek or gall to even think on such a high level.

I could be seen running up and down the stage during one of my talks, comically illustrating to people how to physically visit their goals. To smell the upholstery, watch the destination movies, listen to the stories and just immerse themselves into what they wanted until they believed (with all their heart) that they actually had the power and perseverance to achieve them all.

I would write all my goals down, listing all the steps carefully and in great detail, adding fake deadlines to push me along and excite me like I was taught to do by other goal touters I'd chosen to listen to and be influenced by and in some cases there's some validity to taking your goals seriously. But there's the problem. Why? What is it about setting and achieving goals that's so addictive? What are we trying to achieve? Is there something else at play here? I believe there is.

Big fantasy goals usually have an underlying scent of freedom about them. If we could distil them all down to the essence, what are we really "wishing" for? I think it's the freedom to live a life we choose. That's what's driving us and that's why most of us fail to achieve our goals.

It's not that we or the goals are lame per se. It's just that we use them as symbols for what we really want – freedom. If we can have that massive house, and have millions in the bank, then we'd *have to be* free by default, and it's often not the "thing" we want. It's what it represents and how it makes us feel that we really want.

So why are our goals often so big? Don't get me wrong here, there's absolutely a time and a place for big goals. I love them and I have them. It's just that we often wish for the wrong thing without realising it, which is why we often don't end up getting it because it's not really what we wanted.

What we often really want is the simple freedom to be ourselves. So, if we can twist and mold our thinking to accept that what we really want is freedom, and we can have it much earlier than we thought; we can climb up to that level and start setting physical goals that matter.

Here's another problem with setting goals; they're often dwarfed by what's really possible. By setting goals we run the risk of blocking our potential. Have you ever done something you never thought you could ever do? Would you have ever set a goal to do that? Let me illustrate. During the last ten years I've achieved success on a sometimes fleeting, but spectacular, level.

Here are some real numbers to show you what I mean. I made $10,000 one morning before my coffee got cold (trading options on the stock market). I've sold over half a million dollars' worth of information and training. I've doubled my money in a single day on one stock market trade and in another I made $20,000 overnight. I once sent out one email with an offer to my small email list and sold $67,000 worth of information to very happy customers.

I've lived in multi-million dollar homes. I've had the keys to top-of-the-range Mercedes, Lamborghinis, 40-foot luxury yachts, made $85,000 in one day, sold websites I built for over half a million dollars, and I've written books that changed people's lives. I'm not mentioning these things to brag but rather to make a point. Rest assured, I've had my share of losses and made far too many dumb decisions in the mix to be bragging about anything. My point is this; I would never have *ever* set goals that massive and yet (much to my utter amazement) I achieved them all.

For example, do you think a "normal" person (like me) would have set the massive goal to build a website from scratch, invite people to join for a small monthly fee, enjoy an almost unbelievable passive income often exceeding $20,000 a month, and then sell my share for over $650,000 in just two years? Not in my wildest dreams!

Who sets a goal to make $85,000 in one day? Or to have the skills, cash and guts to make $10,000 a day? No way could I ever – in a million years – have been convinced that (and all those other massive achievements) was even possible, let alone plan it and achieve it – and yet I did it without ever setting the goal. What does that tell us? Was I just lucky or was there something else at play?

The lesson I learned here was to never underestimate the power I had within me to achieve really big things and to never limit myself to what I thought was "reasonable" to imagine. To do so shows contempt for nature and human potential. In that respect, the worst thing you can do is decide what you're capable of. Let natural circumstances decide how awesome you can be – you might surprise yourself.

You don't have enough information to make that decision because you're probably capable of much more than you can imagine so it's counterproductive to set limits in the form of goals you think you can achieve. Inversely, setting massive public goals just to show people how powerful you can be because can be just as damaging to your self-esteem as you might fail to achieve impossible or improbable goals.

Just set goals that you dream of, that excite and drive you naturally (and that you really want to achieve) and work out how to achieve them as you go along.

CHAPTER 22

Lose the Dates On Fantasy Goals!

First, let me clarify what a fantasy goal is. A fantasy goal is something you'd "like" to achieve. Paying the rent by Friday, competing in the 2020 Olympics, making a loan repayment by a certain date each month, getting the contract on a job with an actual deadline are not fantasy goals. These are actual real dated goals with real consequences if you don't achieve them.

What I'm referring to by fantasy goals are things you'd "like" to have or achieve that have no inherent date attached other than the one you decide to attach. For example; *"I want a new car by Christmas"* or *"I must finish writing my book by the 31st of December"* or *"I must become a millionaire by the age of 40"*...etc.

These non-mandatory, manufactured dates have no real meaning, relevance or consequences. There are better and faster ways to achieve fantasy goals than putting fake meaningless dates on them that mean nothing and have no consequences if you miss.

Am I saying that you should just wander around aimlessly through life with no goals or direction at all, just reacting to what happens to you in life? No, but I have an even better suggestion that will feel like strapping freaking jet engines onto your back and soaring higher and faster than you *ever* imagined. You'll be free of restraints, open to natural suggestion and flow with the river of fortune much faster than if you tried to carve your own way through the rock of resistance. There's always resistance so why not go with the flow occasionally? Especially if it helps you get where you want to go faster. Set your sights on a goal. Get as clear and concise about it as you can – get emotional about it and make sure it's something you *really* want but – and here's the magic...

Unleash the power of your fantasy goals by removing your dates and replacing them with A.S.A.P.

This simple A.S.A.P. adjustment will unleash your true potential, supercharge your efforts and dump so much success on you that you're going to be genuinely surprised and humbled. Just let go of the limiting belief that you already know how awesome you are. Trust me; you have no idea how awesome you are. You'd be surprised. You're far more capable of extraordinary feats than you're aware.

It's a very simple thing, and yet the power is surprising and unimaginable. Get a marker or a pen and physically scribble and cross out any dates you set for your goals and replace them with A.S.A.P! Yes, you may keep your original goals and add as many as you like – there's no limit to how many goals you can juggle at once. That's the beauty; nature will take over, and your enthusiasm, curiosity and desire to move in the attractive direction will get you moving along the right path and then – bam!

Nature, circumstance, action and desire all take over, to really sing in unison to produce spectacular results for you! This is human nature given its wings.. and nature loves to fly. Human nature unleashed is an awesome thing. Give it a chance to work for you without self-imposed limitations and you'll see the results much faster than you ever imagined. I know this to be true in my case and have proven it many times over in my personal life.

The reason this works so well is that you're driving towards your goal but you're letting natural circumstance determine your speed. If it's not happening one day – it's not happening. Let it go. To borrow (and butcher) a line from a movie; the goal just "isn't that into you right now." Going with the flow is fine but when you power it with your goal, drive and desire, the thing can travel at light speed. I know this because that's how it happened for me. I'll give you a real example from my own life.

I set a goal to write this book for you. I've been meaning to do it for ages, but the longer I procrastinated, the more experience I was exposed to by discussing these concepts with more people which (I hope) made this a more accurate, relevant and helpful experience.

I tested and validated all these things I'm telling you by sharing them with intelligent people from all walks of life, just like yourself. I've had feedback and taken on good points which (I believe) have actually made this book better. Had I set a firm dated goal to finish this book by a certain date I might have missed out on some vital information that could well have made a large difference to you. By taking "nature's pace" I believe this is a better book.

If you're feeling a bit relieved by removing dates from goals, you're in good company. For the most part, many people I've put this idea to are also feeling very relieved they don't have to play the silly dated goal game. So, in a sense, we get to "eat our cake and have it too" by keeping the original exciting goals and removing the restraints (our fake dates) that were holding us back. They held us back because when we didn't meet the goals on the date we wanted, we felt dejected, like a failure – even if we made adjustments and moved the goal posts we experienced "goal stress". This was counterproductive, made us feel like failures and eroded our self-confidence.

In reality, nothing could have been further from the truth. Just by even setting a goal (even if it had a date), you had decided to make your life – and therefore the world – a better place, and that makes you a winner. You drank excitement and satisfaction, and even if you didn't know how filling they could both be, you felt good just by creating the belief.

Release the power of your fantasy goals by unchaining them from their fake dates, let nature take over, give her a full head of steam, and hang on for a wild ride. You're about to become even more awesome than you could ever have imagined.

Try it – it works and it's fun and if it doesn't work then maybe you didn't really want to achieve that specific goal? Set another one and this time make sure you *really* want it and you want it *as soon as possible*! You'll be surprised how fast you achieve your goals when you really want them.

CHAPTER 23

Your Road to 2X

You may be one of those lucky people who suddenly discover they're already at 2X and that explains why you've been so satisfied and fulfilled in life lately. Maybe you're already living at 2X but aren't happy because your attitude towards money wasn't as healthy as it could be but now that you truly understand what's important to you (and you can manage your money accordingly) you can let go of a whole heap of stress that was in fact completely unnecessary.

However, if you don't already have a 2X level of income, you might be wondering what to do next. Let me make a few suggestions for a pathway to consider. First we set a clear and understandable goal of achieving 2X A.S.A.P. The first step is to define exactly what your 2X level of income needs to be and focus on it so hard that the mere thought of 2X makes you smile and gently nod involuntarily.

The overwhelming majority of entrepreneurs I've interviewed have accepted $1,000 a week as "X" and $2,000 as "2X". If that describes you, you're not alone. If $1,000 a week isn't enough for you just make $2,000 your "X" and $4,000 your "2X" or more – it's your life. Don't mess around with difficult numbers though. 2X is not a lot to ask of the world. Make sure it's a number that makes you smile and make sure it's a nice round number that's easy to remember.

Next, calculate how much you need for a lifetime's supply of tax-paid cash and round it off. If you're happy with $2,000 a week for 2X then set that as your main goal and aim to get there as soon as possible. No disappointments or delays – just as soon as you can. Every day you'll be happy because you're doing something exciting and satisfying to make sure you have a good life every day, so you don't really care when 2X comes – you just know you want it to come. You think 2X would be fantastic and it's a reasonable amount to expect; so far, so good.

You might be thinking, *"How am I going to get to* 2X? *I don't know how to make more money"* to which I hope you'd add *"yet!"* That's stage two. We're still at stage one. Do you remember the shortcut I spoke about earlier? How you can "experience the feeling of 2X just by having it as a saving in the bank?" So…

Stage 1: "Fake/faux" 2X ASAP

If you do nothing else but build and hold onto that little "fake X" buffer for the rest of your life, you'll have removed a lot of financial stress in your life. It's pretty easy (most people can do it) – and remember; even by doing that small, simple, seemingly insignificant thing, you'll actually be experiencing what it really feels like to be a millionaire.

Please remember that nearly all of the pleasure of being a "millionaire" is the feeling of financial relief. I've had this confirmed by some very wealthy people.

Stage 2: Regular Active 2X

It's OK to stop there but if you want (or are lucky enough to) keep growing, the next step after clearly identified your X, is to build up a regular 2X income; how that's done will be different for everyone.

You might be able to achieve it by adjusting your eX(penses). You might be over-spending right now (as a habit which you can break), and could quite rapidly and comfortably get to 2X just by examining your expenses and deciding if they're worth the cost of not having 2X. If they're not, get rid of them and enjoy the relief that comes from having that buffer.

I've heard many real stories of people doing just that; adjusting their way to 2X on their current income and feeling a massive sense of relief in doing so. It's almost like instant wealth if you suddenly realise you're wealthier than you thought.

Stage 3: Regular Passive 2X

I think the next natural step is the most exciting of all. 2X without having to work for it. If you're lucky enough, it might come from real estate investments or you might have built up a partly passive internet income from scratch. However you get there, you can't deny that a passive 2X is right up there with what most people would associate as a "millionaire" lifestyle. Just imagine having every day off from now on, but with a 2X regular passive income. What could you do on a daily basis if you had a $1,000 expense account for the house and bills and an extra $1,000 for fun and luxury? It's a fantastic life. Trust me, it's awesome!

Stage 4: Irregular Cash Injections

OK, so you have a nice 2X lifestyle and life's good. You're not "rich," but you're cashed up enough so you don't have to constantly worry about money or stress about bills. You're free to think and do as you please on a consistent basis and by being free enough from financial stress to think about other ways to make money you've discovered and unleashed more income into your life.

Cash injections are serendipitous events like unexpected or irregular profits; such as small lottery wins, capital gains through sales, bonuses, cash gifts (it happens)... etc. What do you do with irregular cash injections? Nothing! You bank them and you leave them there. Remember, the "Three Pocket" system for managing money? X goes into your left pocket. Another X goes into your right pocket and everything else goes in the bank.

You bank and store *all* income over 2X and you just keep doing that until you have a larger buffer and eventually a "lifetime's supply of cash". Then you can stop – if you like – or you can keep growing to become a millionaire, multi-millionaire, ultra-millionaire, billionaire or even trillionaire.

CHAPTER 24

Never Spend Your Savings!

"For a lifetime supply of $2,000 a week income, I need at least $2 million in the bank earning 5%. What if I want to spend some of that while saving for a lifetime's supply of cash?"

This is a good question. No one ever taught us how to save, how to spend, how much is "enough money", or if there *is* such a thing as "enough money". I think by now we've established that there absolutely is a level of "enough". But are there any rules for how much of your savings you can spend? I've never heard any, so I created some of my own.

Imagine your income has reached more than 2X and you've started to save that extra cash. For example, let's assume you now have $10,000 in the bank and are feeling great – which you should be. Before understanding 2X, it might have been reasonable to buy a reliable car for (say) $6,000 and keep $4,000 in the bank for "emergencies", repairs and insurance...etc. That would have been a reasonably sound decision. Much better than spending all the $10,000 on a car and having nothing left over – right?

However, let's have a look at it from our new perspective. $10,000 at 2X represents only five weeks of reserves (if we use our example of 2X being $2,000 a week). If you become accustomed to the $2,000-a-week lifestyle and suddenly your income stopped (it happens), you'd either have to sacrifice your reasonable lifestyle or risk running out of money in five weeks.

If you had bought that car for $6,000 you'd now only have two weeks of income left! That puts a whole different perspective on money and savings, doesn't it? But let's say you also sold a website for $650,000 (like I did) and, even though you might not have a lifetime's supply of cash in the bank yet, I think it would probably be OK to spend $6,000 or even $16,000 on a car if you *absolutely* had to.

Perspective is the key. $6,000 taken from $10,000 savings is a much larger slice than $6,000 taken from $650,000 savings so use your common sense and some perspective. It's all a matter of perspective and, because you've been so good with money since discovering the 2X method of thinking, no right thinking person would be able to accuse you of being wasteful or irresponsible by spending such a small percentage of your savings.

Don't ever go overboard with spending though. You'll regret it like you always do. As a hard-and-fast, bottom-of-the-barrel decision tool, use this simple formula. Spend no more than one third of your cash reserves at any time on anything and, if you do, it better be important because that's your cash in the bank reserves which are very important because they represent an essential financial buffer.

Yes, of course you would run out very quickly if you spent 1/3 of your savings every single day but I presume we're talking about large and very occasional purchases. Always think long and hard before spending your savings. They're performing a very important task in keeping you safe, comfortable and stress free just by being there.

Never spend more than 1/3 of your savings (cash reserves) on anything!

It's not being wasted and unproductive just by sitting there. It's serving a very important and crucial function. It's giving you (no matter how large it is) a "millionaire's" level of relief. Even if it's only thousands of dollars – it's acting upon your mind with as much power as if it were millions of dollars.

CHAPTER 25
How to Be Wealthy On a Minimum Wage

How far from wealth are you right now? Are you closer than you thought? To write this book I moved into a small one-shop town in a tiny cabin by a lake, far away from modern civilisation just so I could focus on writing this book. While there, I calculated that I only needed $320 per week to live (i.e. my "X" was $320 a week).

Here's the kicker; the minimum wage at the moment (in Australia) is currently $640 a week so I was stunned to discover that I could be a free and feel wealthy simply by earning a minimum wage. I was discussing this with a good friend of mine recently and he had a similar experience working as a truck driver.

His "X" was about $740 a week. With a bit of overtime he often made double that so he very often made "wealthy levels" of income which he told me felt very satisfying. Using just this one small shift in mindset he was able to relax about his financial situation and appreciate how wealthy he actually was.

Perspective is wonderful and powerful. Your expenses are your own and private and you should resist comparing yourself (ever) to how much anyone else has or society's definition of what constitutes a "wealthy" person or lifestyle.

2X is a level that is comfortable for you and you alone. Only you can decide what constitutes financial comfort for yourself. It's certainly not decided by an arbitrary numerical figure such as the popular "millionaire" tag. Understanding the "2X" concept will free you in the blink of an eye and two nods of your head and though it's not "wealth" in the way it's normally been understood and described, it is a very "rich" and free life.

CHAPTER 26

"But I Want a Better Lifestyle Now!"

At this point you might be thinking "Yes, I get all that but Bill, I want a better lifestyle and I want it now! I've got 2X, it's passive (or not) and I've started to build my lifetime's supply of cash but it's a very big number and what if I never get there? Are you telling me that I have to wait until I have a lifetime's supply of cash in the bank before I can move to a nicer house?" No, you don't.

The first success point on your way to substantial financial wealth is to get to 2X using any means you can (passive or active). But let's say you want to move into a better house. Can you do that? Yes, you can. But you must maintain your 50/50 ratio as you grow in order to maintain 2X, so here's how you could do that.

Let's say the "better" house costs an extra $100 a week in rent. Rent is an essential expense so it must come out of your left pocket. In order to fit an extra $100 a week of essential expenses into your left pocket and still maintain your 2X lifestyle, you must set aside an equivalent amount (another $100) for fun and luxury to go into your pocket in order to maintain your 2X balance.

If you notice, by doing that, your essential expenses just become twice as expensive, because not only do you have to find the extra $100 for the higher rent (left pocket essential), you also have to find another $100 (right pocket fun and luxury) for balance.

Alternatively, in order to maintain your 2X balance, that same $100 in extra income could be split equally between your left and right pockets; $50 in each, which means, if you made an extra $100 a week and wanted to use it to improve your lifestyle by moving into a better house you could only afford $50 a week in extra rent and balance it out by adding an equivalent $50 for fun and luxury. This method works very well for spending control.

Keep the 50/50 balance in mind and your financial decisions will always be simple and intuitive.

CHAPTER 27

2X – The Final Word

The 2X Method and formula is beautiful in its simplicity and powerful in execution. It not only offers a solid financial understanding, plan and method of controlling spending and savings, it's also infinitely adjustable, relatively simple to achieve (especially when you compare it to trying to become a "millionaire"!) and easy to maintain, explain, share and teach.

Just a final word about our hypnotic addiction to millionairism as a society; I want you to think about how difficult it would be to actually become a millionaire. Compare the effort required to make $1,000,000 a year to the effort required to make just 10% of that ($100,000 per year) to land at 2X (if your "X" is $1,000 a week as in the example in this book), and how the two compare with regards to providing a very similar sense of security and relief.

Let's compare them to building mounds of earth again. Becoming a millionaire is like trying to build a mountain of earth to live on compared to 2X which is more like building a small hill to live on. The mountain is going to take a lot more effort – in fact, such a massive effort that many give up before "succeeding at wealth".

The small hill is still going to take a lot of effort but it's achievable and, besides, who wants to live on top of a mountain anyway? To stretch the metaphor – it's hard to get there up all the winding roads, its cold at the very top, it's steep and the air is thin. Is it possible that it might be nicer living in a nice house on the hill overlooking the city lights? I think it fits so much better as an analogy with who we are, and by "we" I mean the type of person you are to have read this book.

I believe we all deserve a chance to enjoy abundance because abundance is natural. If having millions of dollars is your burning desire you will get there if you serve enough people with a genuine, generous and sincere desire to help. Having my first "big win" and experiencing that special feeling of freedom was a startling and exciting experience which undoubtedly changed me forever. Through my personal coaching and consultation I've been able to change the lives of many people by delivering the 2X Formula and message and similarly, I hope this book has changed and improved the way you look at money, wealth and freedom.

Using and remembering the 2X formula will allow you to re-discover your own wealth. I wish you well on your journey to financial freedom and beyond and remember;

Financial freedom is closer than you think.

Bill Stacy

Acknowledgment:

[1]Thank you to Tim Ferriss, for allowing me to quote from The 4 Hour Work Week [Vermillion Publishing ISBN 9780091923532]

Notes: